MW00440929

REFLECTIONS

ON TIME, CULTURE, AND SPIRITS IN AMERICA

DENNIS MCCARTY

GENTLE ATHEIST PRESS

This book is for Moira and Quinn. It's really all about them.

AUTHOR'S NOTE

This is not a travelogue, neither is it a scholarly work. It is an array of reflections from the heart.

Upon retiring from Unitarian Universalist ministry in 2015, I treated myself to a three thousand-mile "rolling spiritual retreat" across the western half of the United States. If Reformation theologians were correct and the journey really is the destination, my trek turned into ten days' worth of destination.

I wandered westward, pausing multiple times each day to observe, take notes, and reflect. With regularity, while perusing my road atlas, some tiny, red square whose existence I had not even suspected two days before, would become a place of pilgrimage. I believe one has to know the story of a place and its inhabitants, to appreciate its spirituality. And there are a great many places on a journey.

On returning home, I enhanced my reflections through print media and online research. Anyone can, with a library card and an internet search engine, access any and all data I share here.

Feelings arose and themes evolved. I found myself ever more deeply witnessing to the breadth of the human condition: its oppression, catastrophe, violence, resistance, and resilience. I felt compassion, heartbreak, and dismay, but also awe and amazement. By degrees, engagement gave birth to insight. Of course my laboriously won new insight can also be another person's painfully obvious.

This process felt, in its own way, religious to me. I lamented a human condition I found as often heedless, even criminally so, as it is triumphant. I felt the keen double edge, the Damocles's sword of human creativity itself. Yet such is ardent humanity and the world in which we strive, I found myself celebrating life breathtakingly beautiful in its very precariousness.

In writing down my research and reflections, I chose to augment certain history-based passages with narrative invention. I chose to signify such "imagination added" passages with italics.

PART I
A ROLLING SPIRITUAL
RETREAT

Whoever you are, no matter how lonely, the world offers itself to your imagination, calls to you like the wild geese, harsh and exciting—over and over announcing your place in the family of things.

—Mary Oliver, "Wild Geese"

SEEKING SOMETHING

I was born in the exact middle of the twentieth century, near the geographic middle of the United States. I grew up in the Rocky Mountain West, first in Colorado, then in Utah.

As a post-World War II, Euro-American child, I spent my elementary school years comfortably believing that the word, "American," meant things that were comfortable and familiar to me and mine. As I matured, of course, I learned differently. But even today, sixty years later, I'm still on a journey out of my own egocentric, ethnocentric viewpoint. I still get surprised every now and then.

I wandered far from my mountain roots as an adult, eventually becoming a minister. I happen to be atheist, but within my Unitarian Universalist tradition, an atheist minister is not a big deal. Religion is, for us, about outlook, practice, and relationship. This influences the way I see things—impossible to ignore as I share my impressions.

As my sixtieth birthday faded behind me, I realized I had "lost a step," as athletes put it. Mind and body had grown weary from ministry's day-to-day challenges, the human weight and responsibility of a congregation. I retired from parish ministry at age sixty-five. No less religious for that change, I decided to mark this new phase of my life with what I called, "a rolling spiritual retreat."

I mean nothing magical by the word, "spiritual." Religion is, to me, yearning and openness beyond the reasoning part of the brain. It wants an ear for the poetry, music, and living metaphor of the world, biorhythms, and cosmos unfolding about us. I do sometimes use such traditional religious words, though with non-traditional meaning. Einstein did the same thing. I feel I'm in good company.

The word "spiritual," in my retreat, meant this: I did not know what I was looking for. I was absolutely certain I would find it. Or perhaps more accurately, I was certain it would find me.

I would cross the western United States from my home in southern Indiana to Seattle, where my children and grand-children live. I did not lay out a precise route. I would just read the signs, follow my nose, and adjust my path as new interests rose. I would pay attention, play off what the land itself told me, listen to feelings as they rose within me, and allow my journey to evolve as I went. I would, I felt positive, know and feel and understand something new by the time I was done. And that it would be worth knowing, perhaps even worth sharing.

I purchased a virginal spiral notebook and a brand new packet of pens. I loaded tent, sleeping bag, cooler, and camp stove into my white hatchback, along with laptop, plenty of coffee, and a guitar so I could sing to myself when I got lonely.

I backed out of my driveway in mid-September 2015, my car so full I had only a tunnel to see what was behind me. It would be side mirrors and "be damned careful" all the way. That tingle of risk, I believed, was part of a good adventure.

"The world offers itself to your imagination," poet Mary Oliver writes. Accepting her offer, I planned to drive about six hours per day. That would leave time for tent set-up, cooking, walkabouts, written reflection, and general psychic rewiring. Armed with a road atlas and a National Geographic guide to the nation's one hundred most interesting state parks, I planned to camp most nights. Where campgrounds were sparse, I would rest my bones in a motel. Motels have showers, after all. And internet access.

WIND

To me, Mary Oliver's poem, "Wild Geese," sums up a key religious challenge: to get out of my own head and *pay attention* to where I am and what's going on around me. I wish I were better at this.

When I do so reflect, the focus can be as abstract as galaxies, plentiful as grains of sand. Which makes our relatively tiny earth—let alone one much tinier human being—a grain of sand, cubed. Focus can be as immediate and huge as what happens to an unarmed black youth who comes under the angry eye of a police officer on a big-city street. Focus can even be something as easily taken for granted as the wind.

I think wind is a good place to start. Wind goes everywhere, and was doing so long before the human race came along. I only pay attention to it if I happen to be raking leaves, or perhaps if a storm blows in. Yet when I do stop to think about it I find this: merely to lift my face to a breeze is to touch the hem of eternity's garment. Where I live, in southern Indiana, wind gusts make cornfields undulate and forests sway in elegant quadrilles. But those cornfield-rustling breezes and gusts are born and reincarnated on the other side of our world.

It's reliably fickle, the wind, and subtly powerful. A breeze delights the skin, but a microburst can tear a doughty oak from the center of a grove and throw it down in a thrash of wasted foliage. Hiking through southern Indiana forests after a storm, I may come across a confusion of destroyed trunks. I feel awe that something so tall and strong could so instantly be reduced to tangles and splinters. Within hours, workers will come through with bucket trucks and chainsaws to clear roads and restore electrical power. I've watched this play out more times than I can remember.

Wind is eternity we can feel. Much of the United States lies within a wind belt sailors call the "prevailing westerlies." They sweep the loess plains of China, chase waves across the Pacific, carry Chinese dust all the way to America's west coast. They pick up, cast down, on to the Atlantic, carry rains across Ireland, spread volcanic ash from Iceland to Europe. This tour was going on millions of years before China, the United States, NATO, or the Eurozone ever existed.

On a pleasant day outside my Indiana home, the sun shines down through the leaves. It seems so peaceful, present in each moment, yet eternal across time. What I love about trees is that they have a sense of perspective. They never complain, nor do they plan or have ambition. Yet all the visions of God in all the belief systems I have ever studied or heard about could not be more constant or inspiring than those spreading, cathedral reaches. They sprout and blossom, grow, wither, and fall, same as we do. I walk past trunks cast down by the relentless wind, and ponder my own fate. As a religious atheist, I find myself surrounded by living, metabolizing, sacred text. It opens to enlighten the careful reader. I just have to remember to open and read.

SHATTERED SPRUCE

*O*ne place I'm headed with this, is that as important as my "rolling spiritual retreat" was to me, my life takes place within ineffably grander cycles. It cannot be understood separate from them. I planned a leisurely three thousand-mile journey westward, heading into those prevailing westerlies. Yet the lands I crossed are, in ways, better understood in relationship with that wind. I was just the observer. The wind has been working on the land since long before I, or even the North American continent, existed.

The prevailing westerlies first touch North America not where I started out, but where my journey ended: the state of Washington. So I defer to that ancient force. I begin with the wind on Washington's northwest corner, what it brings, and what that means.

Wind-driven Pacific moisture waters Washington's Olympic Peninsula, literally, by the ton. The so-called temperate rain forests of Olympic National Park receive an average of more than twelve *feet* of rain a year.

Lushly watered treescapes grow into thirty story moss patches. Towering spruce, cedar, and Douglas fir dwarf my

Midwestern hardwoods. Their rain-charged ranks march up mountainsides, festooned with club mosses that hang like immense feather boas. Style statements by trees the size of skyscrapers! It has to be seen to be believed.

Along the road to Olympic National Park's Hoh Rainforest Ranger Station, tourists used to stop and marvel at one of the largest Sitka spruces in the world. Hundreds of years old, it had attained a bulk that loomed so far over my head I couldn't even make out the crown. It was the kind of tree—well, looking at trees like that, all I can say is, "Dang, that's one big tree!" My supply of tree metaphors just doesn't measure up to the task.

Then in December 2014, a storm blew in off the Pacific and snapped off the trunk of that tree thirty-five feet up. The falling bole shattered like an immense vase and left a tall stump, called a "snag," looking down on shards of tree the size of houses. Thirty stories high, twenty feet thick, it had withstood the winds for centuries. Was this one storm that much stronger, I wondered? Or was something else going on?

Sure enough, studying the remains, I could see that except for the outermost shell, the whole tree was consumed by dry rot. This "monarch of the forest" had been dying from the inside out for decades. Even as tourists like me marveled at its magnificence, it had been, you might say, a dead tree walking.

There's a happy ending, though. Such fallen monarchs become "nests of spicery," nurturing forest rebirth in the form of diverse flora and fauna. Birds and squirrels build homes in the snags. Seeds land on the rotting remains and flourish in the richness of the decay. I couldn't walk a mile in this rainforest without coming upon a dozen such logs, many with rows of new trees growing out of them. In the immensity of time, the deadfalls rot down to nothing, leaving new trees' roots standing in graceful arches. Gothic architecture designed by trees. I had to see that to appreciate it, as well.

In this way, the fallen monarch becomes more alive than it was during its final, magnificent decades of verticality. Park botanists gave such deadfalls a charming name: "nurse logs." This is an important thing in my opinion, a kind of communion which calls every being into a common, life-sustaining process.

In its end-of-life decay and collapse, the tree could fittingly have said, "This is my body, take and eat." And the animal and vegetable kingdoms comply, each after their kind. That, I eventually learned, is a key end lesson of my journey. A great tree fosters new life even as its own life fades. If we love the cycles of birth and rebirth, then we must love the demise and tragedy from which, phoenix-like, they arise.

Best of all, what finer calling could there be for a towering tree or for an average retired human? That begged a second question of course. What does a human nurse log look like, what is the job description?

DEADFALLS LIKE JACKSTRAWS

*T*here are storms and there are storms. Following the prevailing westerlies across Washington state, Mount St. Helens stands about two hundred miles southeast of Olympic National Park. The famous 1980 eruption there mowed down old growth trees by the thousands. Deadfalls like jackstraws, billions of board feet. These trees didn't become nurse logs. They were just plain dead.

The numbers seem calculated to astound. The eruption triggered landslides that stripped away mountainside and soil, and mowed off trees for nearly twenty miles in each direction. It blew thirteen hundred vertical feet off the top of Mount St. Helens, a cubic mile of stone, ash, gas, and ice. It snuffed out every living thing across two hundred thirty square miles of the Cascade Mountains. Fifty-seven human beings died, along with thousands of deer, elk, and bear. The economy suffered billions of dollars of damage. And those trees. The tangled trunks washed into river and lake. Their dead, desolate ranks covered mountain slopes like thousands of pick-up sticks. They're still visible from weather satellites.

Growing up in Grand Junction, far western Colorado, geology was part of my earliest education. My mother called herself a "rock hound," and sometimes referred to her children as her "pebble puppies." The Grand Valley's wind-carved plateaus were like open books of earth's history; learning their geology became a family hobby which is still with me. It provided my first insights into the world's interlocked cycles.

Given my own history, Mount St. Helens became a destination early on. It felt like something of a consummation to drive the long, curving highway to Johnston's Ridge, where stands the new visitors center, six miles from the blasted summit. Reaching the freshly striped parking lot, I climbed out of my car, trekked to the uppermost viewpoint, and stared out at the crater. "Wow!" I said to myself. I had read much about the eruption, but now realized I had still underestimated it. Even after thirty five years, the devastation jarringly exceeded pictures and printed accounts.

The crater filled my horizon, a broken, cyclopean bowl a half-day's hike away. Steam drifted up from a newly grown cone, small in the hole where the mountaintop once loomed. Lower down, brush and new trees sprouted along the ashy slopes. Wildflowers had advanced year by year in their gentle battalions. They showed no fear of the still-brooding inferno of magma miles below their roots.

Chipmunks darted across walkways and peeked from under shrubs. I saw whirlwinds here and there, lashing along the broken slope in tight spirals. One danced toward us tourists, whipping up dead leaves and dust, then up over the handrail and past me. Far off to my left, miles away, I could make out the glittering corner of Spirit Lake. It was quite a large lake.

When the mountain began to act up in 1980, geologists

monitored the tremors week after week. From ten miles down, they could track magma working its way up inside the cone. On the mountain's northern shoulder, that pressure bulged a dome five hundred feet high and a mile across. University of Washington volcanologist Dave Johnston made no bones, the mountain scared him.

He was checking instrument readings the morning it all gave way. A landslide tore down the slope toward him like a thousand crazy freight trains. Relieved of the restraining weight, magma burst out sideways, a hell of gas, steam, ash, pumice, and debris. Clouds of superheated gas and ash, called pyroclastic flow, sped downhill, past the landslide. Scientists estimate that Johnston had forty seconds to reflect on his fate, standing about where I was now standing. His last words were a radio transmission edged with fear: "Vancouver, Vancouver this is it." One wonders what he did with his final sliver of time. Did he try to run, or perhaps save the scientific notes he had been taking? They never found his body, only a twisted remnant of the trailer he was working out of. They named the place Johnston's Ridge, after him.

The landslide rolled over that ridge and the next two beyond. It sloshed Spirit Lake into a six hundred-foot wave, so filling the basin that when the water sloshed back, the lake had been lifted two hundred feet! The hot gas and ash went even farther, smothering and burning everything the landslides missed. That's how most of the people died.

The heat also melted the exquisite glaciers which had given the mountain its pre-eruption nickname, "America's Mount Fuji." Meltwater combined with ash and dirt to form volcanic mudslides, called lahars, which swept away houses, broke bridges, and closed the Columbia River to sea traffic a hundred miles away.

The volcanic plume towered miles into the sky—that's

the image people remember. It blotted out the sun over Yakima, Washington, seventy-five miles to the east, and windblown ash covered the ground a hundred miles away. They had to close the east-west freeway between Seattle and Spokane for days.

Gazing down from Johnston's Ridge on this day, I saw three yellow school buses disgorge their lively contents in the visitors center parking lot. Middle school students flowed up the walkway in a human lahar. They seethed with energy, curiosity, a kind of robust heedlessness. I watched one boy drop his pants, "moon" his friends, then yank them back up before a teacher could catch him. He pranced on up the walkway, blending in with a jostling knot of his fellows.

One cluster of kids percolated up to the viewpoint where I stood. A brown-haired girl, perhaps eighth grade, was asking her friends, "Have you seen my iPhone?" They all stopped to read a display, information about the explosion. "I've lost my iPhone," she repeated, plaintively. She and a blonde friend started back down the path to look for it.

Back down at the plaza, a park ranger began a lecture on the eruption. He was a good speaker and plainly enjoyed his bombastic topic. He showed blow-up photos and recited eye-bulging facts and figures. Some kids, the nerds, listened intently. Others fingered their handheld devices, in worlds of their own. Tourists like me gathered around the edges and took notes.

It made a charming tableau, but it also, I thought, said something about our culture. Most of life happens unseen and unheard, because most of us are paying attention to something we just bought. "Yay for the nerds," I thought to myself, "for they shall inherit the earth."

One apparently cannot out-nerd a volcano, however. The ranger explained that of the fifty-seven people killed by this eruption, all but two were at what experts considered a safe distance. Famously, lodge keeper Harry Truman refused to leave Spirit Lake no matter what. Dave Johnston was the other, right at the edge of what was considered the danger zone. All the other victims had thought themselves prudent citizens at a safe, prudent distance. Wrong.

In the long run-up of tremors, small eruptions, and that growing bulge, geologists knew something big was coming. Studying similar eruptions around the world, they thought they knew what to expect. But they hadn't taken all variables into account: gummier magma with more gas and steam content, even the shapes of the canyons and ridges. All these things made a difference. Mount St. Helens was ten times more destructive than any previous lateral eruption. So much for what we think we know.

If I were fated to be killed by a volcano, I would choose Mount St. Helens. A down-rushing immensity of mountain-top, a searing blast of superheated air and gas—not my idea of a good time, of course, but at least quick. That titanic forty seconds, trying to grasp the scope of my fate, but then over in a searing instant.

An internet search on my laptop turned up eruptions that made Mount St. Helens look like a popgun. Yellowstone Park's potential for destruction is all over YouTube, Wikipedia, and more official sites. Over the last twenty million years, super-eruptions from the so-called Yellowstone Hot Spot, a huge trunk of magma which circulates clear up from earth's mantle, have spread volcanic ash for thousands of miles, all across the continent. The last really huge eruption there was six hundred thousand years ago. Miles down the magma still surges, its own kind of life form inside our living planet.

Miles below the daily affairs of humanity's millions,

ancient and immense processes work and wait. Whether one buys the idea of a supreme being or not, geology holds awe enough to galvanize anybody. I believe it's the awe that counts. Our relationship with great magma trunks like the Yellowstone Hot Spot is on earth's terms, not ours. They will have their say in the fullness of time.

DUST

To me, Mount St. Helens serves as a reference point for a whole other league of volcanic conflagration. Big as Mount St. Helens seems, the western United States has an ancient history of so-called super eruptions so much larger, no one even recognized them as volcanic. Only in my lifetime have geologists come to understand how such immense systems work.

Early in my journey, driving through Iowa, I crossed one such prodigy. Following two-lane blacktop through the agricultural heartland, I wouldn't have dreamed that Iowa's heartland took its nature from an ancient volcanic blowout, wind-carried from the west. All about me lay a golden sea of cereal crops. Hilltop forests stood here and there, occasional green islands in the distance. I passed a yard of huge John Deere-green farm machines.

Driving into Sioux City, it seemed as though I saw almost as many churches as tractors. Iowa was a land of traditional faith, I mused, white steeples jutting toward transcendence. But "transcendence" is a loaded religious word to me. They lived right atop a different kind of transcendence, a geological process which made my next stop.

I turned north along the Sioux River, onto the Loess Hills National Scenic Byway. A loamy ridge loomed to my right. Nestled below it, my guidebook informed me, was Stone State Park with soil of remarkable ancestry. If transcendence can be taken to mean depth and reality beyond normal human insight and experience, then I found it in Stone State Park's dust.

Iowa lies within easy reach of the Yellowstone Hot Spot's super eruptions. Time and again over the ages, prevailing westerlies carried titanic outbursts of ash over the land, settling week after week, layers hundreds of feet deep, which snuffed out every living thing for more than a thousand miles. Over more centuries, rainfall would harden such ash deposits into concrete-like stone.

With the rolling of the ages, mile-deep glaciers came crushing out of the north, grinding the petrified ash back into dust all over again. The climate warmed, the glaciers pulled back. Wind re-deposited the dust in new layers, called loess. The Sioux River now cut into a ridge of pure loess, the western edge of Iowa's loess hills. The bounteous farmland I had just crossed was loess. Ahead of me, the Stone State Park's forest-shaded hollows were loess.

Loess covers about 10 per cent of the earth's surface. The loess plains of China, hundreds of feet deep, are world famous. But the loess hills of America's Midwest are nothing to sneeze at (so to speak). People around the world have farmed loess for thousands of years. It still feeds us despite waste, erosion, and human carelessness.

I found the park's campground, chose a campsite, and pulled my tent out of my car. The tent was a little miracle of ingenuity. By this time, three days into my trip, I could unroll it, straighten the braces, add a stake here and a rope there, and have shelter in ten minutes. Throw in sleeping bag and air mattress, more technical marvels, I was sleeping in style, and setting up and tearing down camp in a fashion that would be the envy of those who passed this way centuries before.

It still being bright day, I followed a labyrinth of hiking paths up out of the shade. I found myself once more looking out over that golden sea of grasses. I wandered, took photos, then went back, cooked supper, and hauled my guitar out of my car.

I've found that if I sing and play softly, people hardly ever mind. It's not music anyone would pay to hear, but it drifts through the trees, and more importantly, into my own soul. It's my own little communion with nature and self, a way I drive away shadows and refill empty places in my own spirit.

The next morning I toured a little museum dedicated to the loess hills. One display was designed as a tunnel into the loess, which I descended to find myself surrounded by roots. There were tree roots, cash crops, bindweed, flax, switch-grass, fennel. I peeked down animal burrows carved into the soil. Loess, it turns out, is wonderful stuff in which to build burrows.

Ancient life and death pulverized by glaciers, blown about, and laid back down as fields which now produce the food we eat. There's eternity in that, a kind of palpable, real-world transcendence that does move me. We take living communion each day in the compounds we ingest: dust, rain, bread, lean cattle, fat pigs. We are all endlessly recycled silicates and hydrocarbons.

Carl Sagan quipped that the atoms comprising each of us came from the hearts of exploding stars. He's right, of course, but that is, to me, also distant and general. This natural history of loess was fetchingly specific. I felt content and grateful to be, in that moment, living hydrocarbons.

ASHFALL

I'm a fan of the sciences. They sing of wonders great and subtle, and our ultimate place in things. Astronomy proclaims our tininess before the cosmos, while geology sets human finitude against the vastness of earthly time. The fingers of my imagination cannot close on what a billion years even is. But our world has stirred beneath its crust for multiple billions of years. It's a history grand, violent, and tragic; so huge we can only understand it in the abstract. Our shiny, technological society merely scurries our temporary way across the surface.

I paused my scurrying this evening to read a book on Great Plains natural history. It evoked ancient Nebraska twelve million years ago. It drew an image of *a rolling savanna. Lush grasses sway on the breeze, and willows line a waterway. Bushes hang heavy with berries, birds pipe, bizarre-looking mammals come down to drink. There are camels and three-toed horses no taller than large dogs, also larger, single-hoofed horses. Most striking are the short-legged rhinos, jostling herds of them.*

From the west, a vast cloud creeps over the horizon, implacably covering the sun, like the advancing doom it is. Lightning bolts flash in the blackness. Thunder deafens, the air fills with choking powder.

Thus arrives volcanic dust from the Yellowstone Hot Spot, a form of pulverized, natural glass. Animals cough and struggle to breathe in the dusty darkness. Dying birds drop into the water before they can even land. Leaves sag beneath the dust and it sloughs to the ground in sliding puffs. Mice die, squirrels die.

Day after day, more dust drifts down. Larger animals cough, shake their heads miserably, trudge down to the water to drink. The ash has turned the water to goo. They collapse into the mud, and scavengers tear at the carcasses. Then the scavengers also die in the dust. Largest and hardiest, the rhinos cling to life longer than the others. They come down to the water and stumble over the carcasses of the fallen, breaking the bones of the dead.

The dust powders down for weeks, settles foot on top of foot. Once it does stop, the sun shines on land dead and gray as far as the eye can see. The dust is so deep, the corpses don't even bulge the surface. This is how a world ended twelve million years ago.

Months go by. Rain tipples the dust into gray mud, washes down in rivulets. Seeds blow in, grass struggles up, wildflowers sprout. Decades go by. Grass, brush, trees thrive on the iron-rich dust. Centuries pass. Beasts from afar wander back to a landscape once more come to life. Yards below their feet, volcanic chemicals filter through the petrifying skeletons.

That ash cloud, I read, later became part of the loess I admired in Iowa. It feeds millions now, but it wiped out a whole ecosystem when it first hit.

I left Stone State Park in the morning, and crossed into Nebraska. Prairie hid the poignancy of ages: life and death splayed out beneath the oceans of grass. Several hours, many miles later, I turned off US Highway 20 toward a place called Ashfall National Historic Site. The new road followed Verdigre Creek, a slender stream which had carved deep into grassy swells. Successive bands of geologic time, millions of years, lay along the valley walls. All things living today, I reflected, are just icing atop time's layer cake.

The road opened into a parking lot. It was a quiet, off-season day. Half a dozen vehicles basked beneath the September sky. I decided to use the men's room first, before touring the ashfall area.

Long-legged spiders dotted the concrete walkway. I saw two locked in carnal attachment and stopped, amused. The smaller one (presumably the male?) detached itself and hurried away. I doubted it was worried about the human watching it, or the significance of the hill on which it lived. I've read what often happens to male spiders after mating. They're an excellent protein source for impregnated females. The little fellow was just hotfooting it, trying to stay alive. Such a trivial instant, two small life forms doing what life forms do. Is that what eternity looks like? I wondered.

Downhill from the visitors center stood a low, ware-house-looking structure called the Rhino Barn. Along the walkway, white markers pointed out the different geologic layers and the quarried-out places where researchers had removed fossils. This valley was a fossil hotbed, still not fully assayed. Meanwhile, cattle on the far rim grazed placidly, heedless of the skeletons a few yards below them.

Inside the Rhino Barn lay a tangle of skeletons from that ancient, deadly ash cloud. In the big picture, this was a rare bonanza. Such huge finds are scientifically invaluable, prized by paleontologists. This one was discovered a generation ago when one paleontologist, Mike Voorhies, spotted a skull sticking out of this hillside.

After years of digging and development, prehistoric predator now lay exposed beside prehistoric prey. Juvenile rhinos lay beside their mothers. Skeletons of unborn rhino calves even lay inside the skeletons of their mothers. This was, a marker stated, only a corner of that mass dying.

Scientists chipped away at this find for a generation, so that now, each skeleton is reposed atop its own pedestal. Not counting the skeletons themselves, the scene reminded me of looking out an airplane window, high above the Colorado Plateau where I grew up. Each skeleton lay atop its own little mesa.

A display on the far wall explained the ancient super-volcano that did the killing. Unimaginably huge though it was, it was just one of a series: twenty million years of blow-outs across five hundred miles of Oregon and southern Idaho. North America has been sliding its way over the Yellowstone Hot Spot all that time—an endless supply of magma from hundreds of miles down.

Eons of time, thousand-mile distances, a whole continent drifting west across a pillar of magma the size of Europe. Our earth breathes and stirs beneath us, layers slide over layers thousands of miles wide, dozens of miles deep. Okay. My mind is boggled. Twelve million years ago, the rhinos roaming these plains were just one mortal instant in a pageant immense beyond easy comprehension. Hundreds of millions of years before that, this was the bottom of an ocean.

A white-bearded man leaned against the handrail above the display, chatting with visitors. Assuming that he was a docent, I commented on the spread of skeletons. "It's amazing but it's also quite grisly," I said.

He glanced thoughtfully over the bone bed and tilted his head. "Oh, I suppose it is," he said. A twinkle brightened his expression. "But really, it's more exciting than grisly. You can learn so much from a setting like this. It's a whole ecosystem."

We chatted for a moment. Then, like other visitors, I

passed out through the exit door, back to the swaying prairie grass and endless sky. Only much later, reviewing the site's literature, did I realize I had been chatting with Mike Voorhies himself, the paleontologist who first discovered this fossil bonanza!

Had I known I was going to meet him, I might have prepared better questions. I could have thanked him for his discovery, and for taking time to chat with a mere visitor such as myself.

I have no righteous space from which to lecture the smartphone addicts for ignoring the marvels at Mount St. Helens. One can't "study up" for each chance encounter, and I have my lapses in focus, same as anybody else. My life is full of about as many missed chances like this one, as good catches. Insight is not a flash of genius, not for me, anyway, but accumulated input and a dash of good fortune. Only the umpteenth encounter produces a blinding flash of what should have been obvious all along.

So I thank Mike Voorhies in retrospect. I also didn't yet know, but he embodied the metaphor I didn't yet realize I was looking for. Mike Voorhies, professor emeritus at the University of Nebraska, had found a way to be a nurse log.

On this day, I thank the glaciers, rocks, petrified bones, and the hills of western Iowa. They gave me the wheat in my bread and the lettuce in my salad today. Will some future Mike Voorhies discover our bones long after we're dead? Not likely. That's a lottery hardly any creature wins. I school myself to be humble in this life, and once it's over, give willingly whatever bread gets made from my bones millions of years hence.

I would prefer to be rye. I really like rye. But really, if I'm eaten by a child who lives and loves--and sometime laughs-- that would be honor great beyond expectation.

PART II
FORT ROBINSON

History is written by the victors.
    —anonymous

CROW AGENCY, MONTANA

*O*ne joy of camping was the hour or two I spent reading each evening. Two titles I discovered on a state park bookshelf were *Pretty Shield: Medicine Woman of the Crows* and *Plenty Coups: Chief of the Crows*. A Montana journalist, Frank Linderman, conducted lengthy interviews with both back in the late 1920s. I found their lives, described in their own words, fascinating. I devoured both books, and have read and re-read them since.

Born in the mid-1800s, Pretty Shield and Plenty Coups were not related, but were of the same clan of the Crow Nation. In their youth, their people roamed from the Rockies to the Mississippi drainage. The Crow allied with Euro-Americans against their bitter enemies, the Cheyenne and the Lakota. But once the Euro-Americans had all the land, they put the Crow on a reservation, same as First Nations who fiercely resisted.

In the 1920s, a time when most Euro-Americans viewed indigenous peoples through a thick lens of stereotype, "Sign Talker" Linderman displayed genuine sympathy and interest in Crow life. This earned him rare trust. Now, a hundred years later, I could relax in my tent and be enlightened by their conversations.

Linderman's interviews with Pretty Shield began one March, in the unused schoolhouse at Crow Agency, Montana. A cluster of frame buildings near the Burlington Northern railway and Little Bighorn River, Crow Agency was touchpoint for the two-million-acre Crow Reservation. That may seem like a lot of land, but it was only a remnant of the Crow's former range.

Only through later reading did I learn why the Crow Agency school building was vacant. Led by Chief Plenty Coups, the Crow had persuaded the US government to build a new reservation school near the Pryor River, where most Crow actually lived, a hundred miles away. That was, I later learned, a major accomplishment. The U S government rarely listened to "Indians." Plenty Coups was a cagey politician, though, and they listened to him.

In March, Montana snow lay heaped under the schoolhouse's eaves. Linderman sat with Pretty Shield and a second Native woman, wrapped in blankets against the cold, huddled around a wood-burning stove. Pretty Shield spoke hardly any English, but her friend spoke more. Linderman spoke little Crow, but as his Crow nickname suggested, knew Great Plains Nations' sign language. Between them, using all three languages, they managed a conversation.

Pretty Shield was born in 1857. She began by explaining how her grandfather, a respected Crow warrior, named her for the shield that hung behind his place in his tipi. Then she explained the idea of medicine animals. Every young Crow had a medicine animal, she told him, to teach and protect them. Her medicine animals were the ants, which knew how to work together and take care of one another. This was my first hint of the Great Plains Nations' sense of kinship, not just with one another, but with the natural world about them.

As one example, Pretty Shield told Linderman how the Crow's traditional enemies, the Lakota, made off with her aunt's children in a raid. But Pretty Shield had many siblings. So Pretty Shield's mother gave her to the aunt as a kindness.

One presumes Linderman's eyebrows went up on hearing this. Mine did. But Pretty Shield assured him, it was no hardship for her. Her aunt was loving and she still got to see her mother often. Such boundless caring, she said, was the Crow way of community. Then she said to Linderman, "White people don't know how to do this."

Much of her book deals with the routines and rhythms of life in a Crow village. The women worked hard, scraping hides, drying meat, preparing meals, making clothing. The men hunted or, less frequently, went out on war parties. When war broke out between the Crow and their enemies, that was a time for "making moccasins," she told him. Out raiding, warriors quickly wore out their moccasins.

Her favorite time, she explained, was when her village moved. The women would cook an early breakfast, then take down the tipis and pack. The boys would bring in the village's horses and make travois sleds. A travois consisted of two slender lodge poles, harnessed to a horse, with a stick platform laced between them. The women would load the packs and children onto the platform. The lodge poles would provide a gentle, swaying ride as the horse walked. The women could visit as they traveled. Children would leap off the travois, run about and play, then climb back on when they wanted to rest.

The Crow had many enemies: Lakota, Cheyenne, Arapahoe, even the Piegan, whom Euro-Americans called Blackfeet. The Crow sent out scouts in all directions. Warriors rode at the flanks, watched for danger, "and we women were always watching the men." Linderman reports that Pretty Shield laughed when she said this, and I can picture it. "We Crows were happy when I was young," she says. "We were free. There was plenty to eat. We could laugh back in those days."

Then the white people killed all the buffalo, she said, and forced the Crow onto the reservation. The Crow had to farm and live in log cabins, which they called "square houses." They became hungry, she told him, and confused.

By the time Linderman knew her, Pretty Shield was an old woman. Her daughter had died of white people's disease, now she was bringing up her grandchildren. In my mind's eye, I watch her smile fade as she turns to gaze out a window at the snow-covered plains and bare cottonwood trees along the river a mile away. I see her old eyes grow wistful.

Far beneath the snow, her medicine animals, the ants, wait for spring. Pretty Shield is a nurse log. But winter has been long and cold. Winter for the Crow people—for all the indigenous peoples of North America—has lasted more than a hundred years. I can choose to be a nurse log in my waning years. Pretty Shield had no choice in the matter, she was drafted into it.

INITIATION

I had never even heard of Pretty Shield or Plenty Coups before I ran across their books. I would read Pretty Shield one evening, then turn to Plenty Coups the next. Pretty Shield mostly spoke of everyday Crow life and tales passed down from her elders. Plenty Coups described men's ways. The Great Plains Nations were rigorous hunter-gatherers and warriors.

An arrow is a straight, yard-long stick, feathers on one end for guidance and a thumbnail-size chip of flint, bone, or metal as a warhead on the other. Buffalo are huge animals. To get the arrow head into the buffalo, the hunter would guide his horse with his knees, leaving both hands free to shoot. A rib would deflect even the best shot, so the arrow was aimed behind the ribs, where it could pierce deeply. Galloping at full speed, bumping up against the shaggy prey, they draw the bow and shoot down through the abdomen. The buffalo would die slowly, dangerous until it became too weak to fight. It makes powerful imagery, lean men on surging horses. What courage! What romance!

Or not. Both books are eminently matter-of-fact,

thoughtful because the Crow were thoughtful in their severe way of life. They lived on the brink of, joy, love, war, and death in equal measure, acutely aware of their natural surroundings. Theirs was a breathing, pulsating, lived spirituality which challenges me, reared as I was indoors.

Girls learned domestic skills from their mothers. Boys' education began with running. That, Plenty Coups said, was the first skill for a warrior-hunter. Only later would they learn to ride the horse and shoot the bow.

He described one childhood scene which, for me, captured the ghastly yet poetic nature of his book. One morning while the men were out hunting, the boys were tending the village's spare horses. His grandfather rode up and told the boys to mount horses and follow him. Out onto the prairie they galloped. I can picture straggles of buffalo, placidly watching them from rounded hilltops. Then they topped a rise to find the hunters, two dozen men on their horses, ranged in a broad circle. In the middle stood a wounded buffalo bull, a big one.

This was an initiation, Plenty Coups told Linderman. One hunter had buried an arrow to the feathers in the bull's side. Blood, tinged with yellow fluid, glistened below the shaft. The bull glowered, shook its shaggy head, bellowed its pain. A black hoof pawed the ground, striking grass and dirt into the air.

The teacher told the boys to get off their horses. The bull charged as they climbed down, scattering them like a flock of birds. The hunters roared with laughter. The teacher told them how a cool-headed boy might be able to run up and strike the base of the bull's tail with his bow. Any boy who could do this and not get hurt, he said, "may count coup."

Taken from the French term for "stroke" or "blow," a "coup" was an honor gained in battle. It most often referred to striking a foe without killing him, but there were other ways to "count coup," as well.

Burned by the hunters' laughter, eight-year-old Plenty Coups threw off his shirt and leggings. Naked, he danced toward the bull, knees bent, keeping his weight on the balls of his feet. The bull locked eyes with him. Men on horses could avoid the bull's angry charges. But an eight-year-old boy on foot—him, the bull could kill. Plenty Coups could see the intent in the bull's eyes.

I read the story avidly, imaging the sun hot on the boy's back, the grass lush against his feet. I could visualize the blood dripping from the bull's mouth. When it charges, the bull shakes the ground. The boy leaps to one side and raps the beast's rump with his bow as it thunders past.

The hunters cheered, but the dying bull was still danger-ous. It turned, pawed the ground, charged again. This time, Plenty Coups barely got out of the way. The beast's blood smeared his chest as it knocked him to one side.

I can see the grandfather, beaming with pride as the hunters finished killing the bull. Plenty Coups was the only boy to count coup that day. He would achieve great things, the old man said. At age eight, he still had his child's name, "Buffalo-Bull-Facing-the-Wind," but his grandfather soon gave him his adult name, Plenty Coups. From Crow to English, that would more specifically translate to "many achievements."

Quite a way to get a name, I think to myself. At age eight, I couldn't even count coup on long division. Yet Plenty Coups' description was matter-of-fact. Such life-and-death events were, apparently, just another day in the Crow class-room. I put the book down. The demands of Plenty Coups's culture were so different from my own, I could only try to guess what my life would have looked like, had I been born into his world instead of mine.

THE FUR TRADE

*E*ach morning I would cook a quick breakfast, load my car, and drive. Even on two-lane, there's not a lot to get in your way across Nebraska. Hailing from mountainous Colorado, I had long looked askance at the plains states. Later, when I found myself living and working in southern Indiana, I had to adjust my attitude. "Any damn fool can appreciate the mountains," essayist Wendell Berry once said. "You have to have an eye for subtlety to appreciate the plains."

I learned over the years there's real insight to Berry's statement. Now, as I drove, the endless grassland spoke to me of time's immensity. It spoke of the way perseverance and determination have to keep a person alive through times when the world's indifference will starve even the most beautiful dreams and visions.

Thus pondering, I drew near the town of Chadron in the northwest corner of Nebraska. A low building with a red tile roof caught my eye. Zigzag letters, faux Native style on a stagey-looking sign out front, proclaimed it the Museum of the Fur Trade.

I'd never heard of the place. The sign recalled any number of tourist traps past, geared to separate me from my money with no insight or inspiration gained. Checking my road atlas, though, there it was, a little red square on the south side of Highway 12. It was a hit-or-miss decision, made in a moment. But I opted to take a chance.

I walked through painted doors into a long, low room of wood paneling and glass display cases. As standard practice, I ignored the small gift shop off to the left. Admission was five bucks. I paid the ramrod-straight woman behind the counter and walked in.

The first thing to catch my eye was case after case of historic firearms. There were hundreds of them, from oiled, polished historical gems to rusting relics. As a scion of the mountain west, I grew up around guns. They still interest me. Many of these were so-called "trade guns," mass produced for fur traders to swap for hides. They ranged from muzzle-loading flintlocks to newer caplocks, to quick-firing Henry repeaters, which were state-of-the-art in the late 1800s.

Displays traced the history of the early French voyageur fur trappers, followed by later European movement into North America. I studied the trade blankets, pots, pans, and ornamental items. Some showed how First Nation clothing changed after exposure to European culture: European-style jackets and shawls, even rifles, all with distinctive beadwork, medallions, or buttons added as decoration.

Above my head, huge voyageur canoes hung from ceiling beams. I was used to the lithe, narrow hobbyist's canoe I have in my own garage: two passengers if your balance is good. These things were thirty or forty feet long, and a man's-height wide. They bore eight or ten people plus weapons, supplies, and bales of trade goods.

It dawned on me that this was what multinational

commerce looked like four centuries ago. Furs and hides became a European cash resource, particularly for luxury clothing. The voyageurs were the first Europeans to set eyes on much of North America's interior. For their commercial backers, European blankets, clothing, cookware, and weapons were concrete investments in a growth industry. Fur trapping and trading pried the continent open to exploration, then occupation.

Beyond utility, indigenous people found European goods exotic, thus items of interest and prestige. Indigenous fashion soon incorporated European motifs. Indigenous hunting, cooking, and warfare utilized western steel, including rifles.

One other thing that revolutionized life on the plains was, of course, the European horse. As escaped horses spread across the continent, plains hunters became more mobile than they had ever been. An indigenous man's horses quickly became the mark of his wealth.

As the fur trade stretched west toward the Rocky Mountains, it became a profitable sideline for Lakota, Cheyenne, and Arapahoe. In the process, trading for long-range weapons first, they could more effectively make war on the Crow.

I spent more time than I planned to, admiring the displays. Then a path out behind the building led to a replica of the trading post set up in the mid-1800s, by an entrepreneur named James Bordeaux. It was a nondescript, sod-roofed structure, dug into a low hillside and stocked with rifles, steel traps, blankets, and coats. In the 1840s, I read, Lakota and Cheyenne would arrive in the spring by thousands, then camp, and trade their winter hides for Bordeaux's goods. It was, at first, a healthy business relationship. Bordeaux got ahead and his customers got ahead. He even wound up marrying two Lakota sisters.

The Lakota and Cheyenne were shrewd, hard-nosed bargainers. They knew their furs' value and the difference between a cheap blanket versus good material which would hold up through many winters, or between cheap iron that would break versus a steel blade that would hold an edge. They insisted on a good return.

I don't think I could have found a more pointed introduction to western Nebraska. The prairie keeps its secrets, silent beneath the timeless sky. It doesn't hint at generations of migration, struggle, life, love, and death through thousands of years before my ancestors even heard of these reaches.

Feeling appreciative that I had stumbled across this gem, I stopped by the counter again on the way out. "I didn't know what to expect when I came in," I told the woman. "But this is really a serious, major-league museum, isn't it?"

She didn't crack even a ghost of a smile. "Yes, it is a serious museum," she said. I felt a bit put off. Only later did it occur to me, she'd probably heard the same thing from other casual tourists, and no longer took it as a compliment. Life is, once more, a hit-or-miss thing. A spot decision whether to engage or how deeply to engage can fuel unexpected journeys. I would benefit from this stop. But had my 52 – 48 percent decision been *not* to walk through those doors, it would have been otherwise.

FORT ROBINSON

*T*he very core of my rolling spiritual retreat was to follow inclination and new information wherever they happened to lead. Witnessing to geology and natural history was one thing. But in western Nebraska, I began to witness how all-too-human spirits clashed and hurt one another on this continent.

My childhood experience never called me to ponder people who lived and died here before my ancestors came. Well, except for TV, movies, or as an abstract exercise. But everywhere I looked, the land expressed, in stark relief, First Nations driven before the onrush of what Euro-Americans glibly called Manifest Destiny. Insight is a matter of accumulation to me. I checked into a Chadron motel that evening, and fired up my laptop to delve more deeply into what I had glimpsed at the Museum of the Fur Trade.

Bordeaux and his Native trading partners had a good thing going, or at least they thought they did. What they didn't understand--what no one fully understood for a long time, indigenous or European--was that the land itself was more dear than any trade that crossed it. Word of farmland spread east. Europeans surged west. They brought European diseases, livestock, and machines. Disease was really the most effective European weapon, killing far more indigenous people than weapons ever did.

The American Civil War brought only a pause. Then came railroads, prospectors and settlers. Then the army moved in. In 1868, the US government worked out a treaty with the Lakota, Cheyenne, and Arapahoe. Euro-Americans got increased scope for settlement where First Nations had formerly roamed freely, but now could not go. First Nations retained "ownership" and hunting rights over a broad swath of what is now South Dakota, Wyoming, and Montana, including what we now call the Black Hills. Worth noting, the Lakota had only recently wrested much of this land from the Crow, who were supposedly Euro-American allies. No matter. The Crow got no say.

There was, as always, the promise of supplies to tide the displaced First Nations through lean times. The supplies would be issued partly through the Red Cloud Agency, near the bluffs of Pine Ridge, a few miles from the old Bordeaux Trading Post.

The ink was barely dry on said treaty when an army column led by George Armstrong Custer, no less, entered the Black Hills. They were officially there to survey. But even though it was officially illegal under the treaty, they prospected on the side. Unofficially, the government hoped to discover gold, provoke a Lakota revolt, and have an excuse to exterminate more "Indians."

It worked like a charm. They did find gold. Custer, a master at self-promotion, trumpeted the news to newspapers. Fortune hunters streamed in and tensions skyrocketed. When a clerk got killed at the Red Cloud Agency, the government sent the army to maintain order. They set up camp nearby. Stone and brick gradually replaced canvas and wood, and they called the place Fort Robinson.

To white settlers, prospectors, gamblers, prostitutes, preachers, drifters, and camp followers, Fort Robinson meant haven, security, and profit. To the Natives, it was a tumor which could not be excised. It still stood, a few miles down the road from my motel room. Now it was Fort Robinson State Park, with a compelling write-up in my National Geographic Guide.

Back in 1872 Bordeaux sold his trading post to a fellow named Francis Boucher, who married the daughter of an important Lakota chief, Spotted Tail. Sympathetic to the Lakota, Boucher supplied them with high-grade arms and ammunition. Reading about him, I think he had higher motives than just profit. Better rifles meant a better life for an indigenous hunter. Boucher provided the best, including quick-firing Henry repeating rifles, like the ones I'd admired at the Museum of the Fur Trade. Years later, the army caught Boucher with a warehouse full of Henries, along with forty thousand rounds of ammunition, and put him out of business. That would be too late for Custer and the 7th Cavalry, though.

Meanwhile, on the far side of the Atlantic, those were Irish-famine years. My great-grandfather, Tom McCarty, took work on a merchant ship. He may have left a family behind in Ireland. Family stories whisper of that scandalous possibility. "Divorce, Irish style," I've heard it called.

When his vessel docked in Philadelphia, my grandfather "jumped ship," as family legends describe it, and drifted west. Regardless whether he left a grieving spouse in Ireland, he married an American woman named Sarah Ketchum. They heard rumors of free land in the West, one hundred sixty acres to everyone willing to farm it. So they wagoned out to the Republican River area of southern Nebraska, and took up dry-land farming.

Indigenous culture and dry-land farming both are about as far as it gets from my own time and citified experience. But some human realities gleam through the dry air of written history. My great-grandparents and the other settlers could not have survived on the plains without places like Fort Robinson.

I resolved to visit Fort Robinson. But as a blue-eyed, blonde-haired Irish American, I would approach it as a place to be thoughtful and humble about my heritage. My ancestors came as foreigners to farm land from which indigenous peoples had been driven. Poor though they were, my great-grandfather's people were of the occupiers. I am colonialism's heir.

I also feel circumspect using the word, "Sioux," to describe the First Nations most affected by Fort Robinson. The several branches of the Lakota, Yanktonai, and Santee peoples to whom it refers, explain that it's not their word. It comes from their enemies. Many find it derogatory.

CRAZY HORSE

*C*hilly mist floated across the late September morning as I drove west out of Chadron. The road stretched before me, straight and gray. An hour later, pale bluffs loomed out of the mist, thatched dark with ponderosa pine. This was, I later learned, was Pine Ridge. Below that sandstone brow lay Fort Robinson, a sprawling horseshoe of nineteenth century military buildings.

Preserved cavalry forts dot America's plains. Fort Robinson followed the standard plan: barracks, stables, officers' quarters, headquarters, all ranged in a U-shape around a parade ground. It was larger than others I've visited.

My guidebook told me to begin at a big stone barracks building, which was now the Fort Robinson State Park Lodge. Cold bit through my sweater as I climbed the steps. My heels drummed across the old pine deck, reminding me of western movies from my childhood.

A friendly white woman behind the counter equipped me with brochures and a map photocopied onto letter-size paper. She circled points of interest with a pen. "You'll have to go next door and see our Trailside Museum," she said enthusiastically. "It's closed today, but come back this afternoon. If the mist burns off, there'll be painters working. They'll let you in. You have to see our Columbian mammoth."

I filed that in the back of my mind, accepted her map, and set out to explore. Built in the days of the Red Cloud Agency, Fort Robinson's history went on long after the "Indian Wars" ended. It even became a prison camp for captured German soldiers during the Second World War, I read.

The grounds were eerily quiet on that morning. I got out of my car near a two-room cabin with iron bars on the windows, a replica of the fort's original guardhouse. Twenty feet from the door stood a small monument which, I read, marked the place where the legendary Lakota war leader, Crazy Horse, was killed, September 5, 1877.

I have read accounts of the killing and seen a line drawing produced by a witness. Now, standing beside the marker, I glanced around at grass, trees, arching sky. The breeze chilled my face. The guardhouse door stood open before me. A running man would cover that distance in a couple of strides.

Crazy Horse was ten years older than Plenty Coups. Crazy Horse's hopeless wars against the army made him famous, while Plenty Coups' facile negotiations with the whites languish in obscurity. That's how legends work, I conclude.

Apart from the rush of battle, which he loved, Crazy Horse was a loner who preferred mystical visions to mundane socializing. The Lakota holy man, Black Elk, described him as "a queer man [who] would go about the village without noticing people or saying anything." "All the Lakotas like to dance and sing," Black Elk tells us, "but [Crazy Horse] never joined a dance and they say nobody ever heard him sing."

The story goes that at a Sun Dance in his honor, after he defeated the white soldiers at the Rosebud and the Little Big Horn, Crazy Horse would not dance. Warriors of distinction entreated him, but he declined. He did not sing or dance or deal in common things.

Plenty Coups was a leader in the traditional sense, a "shirt-wearer" and "pipe carrier" many times over, to use his people's terminology. Crazy Horse led not through office, but through charisma and audacity in battle.

Lakota warriors typically wore a feather for each coup they counted, but Crazy Horse did not bother. He had counted more coups than there were feathers. Instead, he painted a lightning bolt on the side of his horse, white spots to represent hailstones on his body, and went into battle all but naked.

Now here I was, I thought to myself, touching the rough monument, pondering the fallen legend. But legend or not, Crazy Horse was made of real flesh and this was where he died. His blood once stained the grass at my feet.

Crazy Horse annihilated Captain Fetterman and a company of soldiers on the Bozeman Trail. He defeated General Crook and a thousand men at the Rosebud. A week after that, he wiped out Custer at Little Bighorn. But he was only human. By 1877, he was exhausted from ten years of war against ever growing numbers of soldiers. His followers were even more weary. After the Custer battle, many drifted back onto the reservation. A few lucky ones got jobs working for the army. The rest settled for the meagre supplies the government would provide.

Crazy Horse's wife was dying from tuberculosis, another white man's disease. Nine months after destroying Custer, Crazy Horse relented from warfare and joined his brothers and sisters at the Red Cloud Agency. Whites hated him and he hated them. He camped with his people amid deepening clouds of intrigue and misunderstanding. For months, Crazy Horse's men and the white soldiers glared at one another like Achilles and Hector, glaring at one another across the walls of Troy.

As historian Kingsley Bray notes, Crazy Horse's tragedy was that the politics with whites--or even with his own fellow chiefs--were infinitely more taxing than greatness in battle. Where Plenty Coups excelled at such politics and diplomacy, they grated against Crazy Horse's need for privacy and spiritual time. He became moody. Some Lakota leaders began to see him as erratic.

General Crook sent orders for Crazy Horse to be arrested. To that end, Crook transferred more soldiers to Fort Robinson. When Crazy Horse's people saw the reinforcements, they broke camp and scattered. The army tracked Crazy Horse to another agency a day's ride away, and sent officers to persuade him to return and negotiate. At last he agreed. Not knowing the army meant to detain him, he and his lieutenants rode back to Fort Robinson. Other Lakota joined them, including a chief named Little Big Man, who had once been Crazy Horse's friend. Now Little Big Man saw advantage with the white soldiers.

As Crazy Horse entered the guardhouse where I was now standing, a reservation Lakota shouted an insult at him. Crazy Horse saw the iron bars and leg irons, and smelled a filthy chamber pot in one cell. He tore himself away and ran out the door. According to witnesses, an officer grabbed Crazy Horse by one arm and Little Big Man grabbed the other. Soldiers yelled, "Kill the bastard." While the knot of men wrestled, a sentry drove a bayonet into Crazy Horse's back once, then again. Crazy Horse fell. In agony, he grimaced up at the Lakota men standing over him, "Let me go, my friends. You have hurt me enough." He died that night.

Family members managed to spirit his body away from the soldiers. Where they disposed of his remains is a secret his descendants keep to this day.

We could argue whether his killing was a misunderstanding or just plain murder. Today, everyone sees Crazy Horse as a brilliant warrior and hero. They name rock 'n' roll bands and bars after him. Famous actors play him in movies.

In 1877, though, Crazy Horse's victories were still called "massacres." Once General Crook got his hands on Crazy Horse, does anyone really think he would ever walk free again? White America, particularly the US Army, looked on Crazy Horse the same way twenty-first century Americans look on Osama Bin Laden.

In its own way, that makes Fort Robinson the Guantanamo of the plains.

A hundred miles north of that guardhouse, the Crazy Horse Memorial Foundation is using dynamite to "carve" an immense statue of a generic "Indian" out of the Black Hills. They call it Crazy Horse, and brag that the head alone will dwarf the four presidents on Mount Rushmore, all put together.

Musing on this, I can't imagine a more stark juxtaposition of Euro-American spirit versus Lakota spirit. The US Army, the settlers—probably my great-grandfather--all wanted Crazy Horse dead. Now developers plan a visitors center and an educational and cultural center, all named after him. My forbears may have hated Crazy Horse during his lifetime. But that doesn't preclude turning a profit on his name one hundred fifty years later. The commercial spirit is omnivorous. It's not intentionally cruel, I don't think, but sometimes it comes to the same thing.

In fairness, the memorial's founder, Korczak Ziolkowski, was urged to the project in the 1940s by a Lakota elder, Henry Standing Bear. Today, though, it's controversial. No one asked Crazy Horse's surviving relatives, many Lakota say. There was neither tribal consensus nor input on the design, place, or manner of the work. It's a completely Euro-American concept. Finally, the Lakota say, there's the violated sanctity of the Black Hills themselves. The Black Hills are for prayer, not for tourists.

As a Euro-American, I only know a bit of Lakota culture, and for that matter my own Irish forbears, through reading. But how knowledgeable do I have to be to understand that Crazy Horse detested the white soldiers and the settlers and prospectors they protected? He was a loner. Apart from the heat of battle, he hated crowds.

I don't know Korczak Ziolkowski's motivation either, or whether, by his own rights, he was doing the "Indians" a kindness by bestowing a European-style monument on them. Or just building his own career. Or both. In the end, I couldn't see how the Crazy Horse Memorial had much to do with the real person whose blood had stained the grass at my feet. Pondering these things, I decided to give the Crazy Horse Memorial a pass.

DULL KNIFE

*R*eturning to the Trailside Museum with its Columbian mammoth, I found it still locked. I decided to follow a scenic drive that traced its way up one corner of my park map. Horse-drawn wagons carried visitors up this road during tourist season, I read. But this was late September, so I was on my own. I turned up the road, crossed a cattle guard, then drove past a large sign which informed me I was entering a wildlife sanctuary. Don't bother the buffalo, it said. They're dangerous.

The mists had lifted by this time, but the sky remained gray. I wound my way up a jagged gorge that bore signs of an old range fire. Grass grew up the craggy slopes in yellow waves, with fire-blackened brush in bold relief against the yellow. Dead ponderosa pines also bore mute testimony to past conflagration.

Some of the burned trees had toppled. Twisted limbs reached up as though they died writhing. Where flame hadn't blackened the wood, time had weathered it steel gray. Time always wins, I reflect. These canyon walls with their slashed gullies and dead, naked trunks seemed particularly chiseled by time. Trees have a sense of perspective. They don't quail before the inevitable. Still, I would not have envied these their wait as the fire's first smoke wafted toward them.

My little car labored up the canyon, climbing past the silent trees. I knew I was following the park's wagon-tour route because horse turds dotted the asphalt. Here where it was steep, the horses plainly had to work hard.

Toward the top I saw a Nebraska Historical Marker beside the road and pulled off. "Fighting in the Buttes," the caption read. The US Cavalry had chased fugitive Northern Cheyenne up here, then cornered them a few miles west of this spot. This, I later learned, was a famous episode in the "Indian Wars," later memorialized by no less than the great Hollywood film director, John Ford. Ford left the most troubling aspects out of his movie, though. "Fighting in the buttes" was one of them.

On a freezing November morning five months after the Lakota and Northern Cheyenne destroyed Custer, a thousand vengeful cavalry swept down on a sleeping Cheyenne village. This was standard strategy, Custer favored it as well. Chiefs Little Wolf and Dull Knife managed a fighting retreat, and most of the hastily roused Cheyenne got away. But the soldiers burned their supplies and tipis, and captured the Cheyenne's horses. This, too, was standard procedure.

Without lodges, food, or blankets in the bitter cold, Cheyenne babies froze to death in their starving mothers' arms. Dull Knife watched three of his own sons die. Desperate, the Cheyenne surrendered. They hoped to go share the Lakota Reservation under the terms of the 1868 Treaty. Instead, the army escorted nearly one thousand of them south to what was then called the Indian Territory in what's now Oklahoma.

Resources in Indian Territory were stretched thin by the thirty-odd First Nations already confined there. There was no hunting, the buffalo had been slaughtered already. Little was left to feed all those new mouths.

For a year and a half, the Northern Cheyenne languished. Many died from starvation and disease. Finally, Little Wolf and Dull Knife fled the reservation with three hundred desperate followers. They struck north toward their homeland, killing cattle and sheep for food, robbing farms for supplies. Ranchers and drovers inevitably defended their holdings. That got some of them killed. Outrage and consternation swept the plains, and thousands of soldiers and civilians took up the pursuit.

The determined spirit by which this dwindling band of Cheyenne pressed on, not to mention the tactical genius by which they eluded thirteen thousand soldiers and ranchers out to kill them, make me proud to be human. The fact they had to, does not.

Persecuted to ferocity, the Northern Cheyenne were fighting for survival. Individually, the settlers were innocent enough. In the economic recession of the 1870s many of them were driven west by their own necessity. They, too, just wanted to feed their families. Most soldiers had enlisted for employment, food, bed, and board. "Fighting Indians" was just a job. As Custer showed, sometimes it was a dangerous job.

In other words, it was an all-too-human mess. That said, relief for Euro-Americans inexorably came at drastic expense to the land's original occupants. How do you stack individual innocence, even heroic spirit, against collective guilt?

The First Nations' demise has been called genocide, of which this so-called Cheyenne Exodus was one crystallized instant. Moving north, the Cheyenne crossed into Nebraska just west of where my great-grandfather homesteaded. I wonder what rumors flew in that region and how long they lingered. Those details were not passed down in family lore.

The Cheyenne were, by this time, exhausted. Dozens had been killed. They split up. Little Wolf led half toward Montana, Dull Knife led the rest toward Pine Ridge and the Red Cloud Agency. Alas, soldiers surrounded Dull Knife's people before they got that far. In a blinding October snow-storm, his band of Cheyenne surrendered again, but defiant warriors took their guns apart and hid the pieces in the women's clothing.

Instead of the Red Cloud Agency, the soldiers brought them to Fort Robinson and housed them in an abandoned barracks. Dull Knife pledged peace if only the army would let them go to a reservation in the north. The fort's comman-dant did pass that request on to Secretary of the Interior Carl Schurz. Schurz and his military advisor, General Philip Sheridan (who coined the saying, "The only good Indian is a dead Indian,") refused. The Cheyenne would have to go back to Oklahoma.

They responded that they would rather die. Considering them less than fully human, the army was happy to oblige. They installed iron bars on the barrack windows and doors, cut off all rations, and proceeded to starve the Cheyenne into complying.

Fort Robinson really is the Guantanamo of the Plains. With frostbite.

On the night of January 9, 1879, the Cheyenne reassem-bled their concealed rifles and broke out of their prison. Soldiers quickly recaptured about half, killing some and wounding dozens more. The rest scaled the bluffs west of the fort, and fled. Even without horses or provisions, they managed to elude capture for two weeks.

When the army finally cornered them, the Cheyenne dug a defensive position along a ridge. Soldiers charged repeatedly, firing down on the men, women, and children in what came to be known as "The Pit." All but a few were killed. The soldiers suffered casualties, as well.

Only about ten of these Cheyenne survived to at last return to Montana. Remarkably, for he was an old man by this time, Dull Knife was one. He died in 1883, age seventy-five. That same year, my grandfather, Pat McCarty, was born, not far from where Dull Knife's tracks had melted into the Nebraska snow.

The historical marker called this episode, "Fighting in the Buttes." Other sources call it the "Fort Robinson Massacre" or the "Tragedy of The Pit." John Ford's sanitized epic, *Cheyenne Autumn*, doesn't mention it at all. It's a messy detail he decided to leave out. In the movie, which at age fourteen I just loved, Secretary Schurz promptly and compassionately gives the Northern Cheyenne a reservation of their own. No massacre, no freezing to death in the Nebraska winter. Welcome to Hollywood.

Meanwhile, my great-grandfather was unable to make a go of their homestead on the Republican River. Different soil, far less rain than he knew back in Ireland. So Tom and Sarah pulled up stakes and returned to eastern Iowa with their children, abandoning land the Lakota and Cheyenne had struggled so hard to keep. One of their children died on the journey back. After they built a new homestead in Iowa, another died from burns sustained in a fire.

My thoughts struggled to fly in this place, like a broken bird.

SURVIVANCE

I drove along a long ridge, prairie stretching away on both sides, grasses swaying forever under heaven. The vastness shot home to me all over again, my grain-of-sand relativity. Planets, stars, galaxies, local group, galactic super group—anyone can do the cosmic hierarchy. A single human being disappears fast.

I'm a grain of sand, cubed, one temporary human being among billions. Yet each human said grain is a wondrous, living mechanism with feelings just as profound as mine. Multitudes crossed this land ten thousand years ago, each living a story as deeply felt as my great-grandfather's or mine. That's a lot of sand, a lot of emotional energy drained into this vast soil. As I learn the stories, that energy affects me.

Tom McCarty arrived, unapproved, on these shores while unrest seethed in Europe generally and famine in Ireland specifically. All poignantly felt. I don't know if I'd care to meet my great-grandfather. We don't know who or what he ran from, or what crimes he might have committed. We do know he would hide whenever visitors came to his farm. He never allowed his photograph to be taken. When he died it took the local newspaper a week just to learn his name for the obituary. But he and his offspring could travel where they wanted. They sure had it over Dull Knife and those hunted Cheyenne.

Returning to my own time, proceeding on, I found another marker which cheered me up. As it turns out the range fire that burned all those ponderosa pine took place in 1989. Over the following years local Boy Scouts planted fifteen thousand new trees. A generation later, I could enjoy the thousands of saplings that greened spaces between the dead trunks. It was a new and palpable consecration of life in that seared land.

Dammit, I say to myself, there is goodness in the human heart! Sometimes we do bad things, but sometimes we also care enough to restore what's been broken, and the restoration itself is the only reward we ask.

To gloss over the suffering of Dull Knife's Cheyenne is to commit genocide all over again. But farmers and cowboys who got in the way of the Cheyenne's undeniably epic journey also died.

But the Boy Scouts planted trees. Much more, the Lakota, the Cheyenne, and other indigenous peoples, displaced by industrial white culture, managed to survive and retain their identities. Their stories also emanate out of these grassy swells, triumphs of the spirit to inspire and educate in their own way.

A year after this trip, I attended a panel on intercultural dialogue. An indigenous speaker brought up a word that was strange to me: "survivance." Survivance, she explained, is a combination of "survival" and "resistance." I later delved into the term, and found it has a long (and rather obscure) legal and philosophical history. But for me, the most useful and powerful definition was the one I heard first.

In hanging onto their traditions and sense of who they were, in not dying out, in not giving up their language and cultural identities, the Cheyenne and Lakota express survivance. So do many First Nations across this continent. May survivance be honored. May I, and those who look like me, take a moment to ponder what survivance means in our own history and present. May we look for ways to share our inheritances, descendants of survivors and descendants of occupiers. All this may seem abstract, like $E=mc2$. But that equation became real, for both good and ill, in my generation.

Meanwhile, I came to a junction where the park road rejoined US Highway 20. A road sign labeled this stretch of US Highway 20 the "Crazy Horse Memorial Highway." I decline comment.

COLUMBIAN MAMMOTH

*H*alf an hour later, back at Fort Robinson, I parked in front of a white stone building of early twentieth century architecture. This was the Trailside Museum. It was closed for the season I'd been told, but workers might let me in. Alas, there was not a soul in sight. I climbed the front steps anyway, tried the door, and to my joy found it unlocked.

I stepped through and found myself staring up. Massive forelegs and huge, curved tusks loomed over me. A cheery female voice said, "Come on in. Do you like our Columbian mammoth?" A blondish woman in a brown sweater sat at a high desk behind the mounting, smiling down at me.

"Very impressive," I replied. "But I thought you'd be closed."

"Oh, we are," she said with a laugh. "They said you wanted to see the mammoth, so I left the door unlocked." Gracious and enthusiastic, she put down her work and took time to show me around. The display area occupied the whole ground floor. She described each exhibit right up to the stuffed bison in the loft, shot by Buffalo Bill Cody himself.

She was most proud of the mammoth, though, and justly. It dominated the room. Thirteen feet at the shoulder, Columbian mammoths were the largest elephant cousin. This was a complete specimen: massive bones and huge ivory tusks, the framework for its multi-ton mass. One tusk had snapped off three feet from the base. The break was worn smooth, showing that the mammoth had lived a long time afterward.

Then she showed me a sprawling, horizontal display that took up most of the space behind the mounted skeleton. It was a reconstruction of the original fossil find, not just one mammoth, it turns out, but two!

Scientists' best explanation was that two bull mammoths got into a fight over a female more than ten thousand years ago. They were evenly matched, right down to each one having a broken left tusk. Those matching breaks turned a simple pushing match between alpha males into a death trap. In the course of shoving and twisting, they pushed up close and found themselves locked together, eyeball to eyeball, unable to separate.

This still happens with members of the deer family in our own time. Bucks joust fiercely during breeding season. Sometimes two lock antlers, then they're in real trouble. If they can't break apart, they're at the mercy of predators or just plain starvation. Picture that with two eight-ton mammoths and here we are. One mammoth apparently stumbled and fell. That pulled the other down with it. There they both lay until they starved to death and for the next ten thousand years thereafter.

Fast forward to 1962. Who should wind up investigating this find but our old Ashfall Fossil Beds acquaintance, Mike Voorhies. He was just a University of Nebraska undergraduate back then, completing a degree in paleontology. Talk about stumbling into a bonanza! I smiled to think of it.

"We knew right away it was an elephant," Voorhies later reported. Only upon further excavation did they realize they had not one, but two complete skeletons, still locked together in primal battle. "It was probably the most exciting fossil I've ever seen," he told interviewers. That's saying something.

I don't know much about paleontology, I just look at the pictures. University of Nebraska professor emeritus, Mike Voorhies, is now nearing the end of his work. He has added to our understanding of eternity. To me that includes awareness of our own tininess before that eternity. I'm happy just to have met him and read the story.

Perhaps the most relevant comment, though, came from Erin, the elder of my two daughters in Seattle. In a phone conversation a couple days later, I told her about the display. Erin has an earthy sense of humor. Concerning the mammoths' demise she quipped, "That's boys for you. You guys can't breed and think at the same time."

I'm still thinking about that one. Awe and magnanimity do have a hell of a time keeping up with primal drives. Being mammoths, I'm sure neither of these two wanted to be famous ten thousand years later. Or amaze Mike Voorhies. Or help my daughter exercise her acid wit. They both just wanted to show who was boss, and get laid.

I don't know if they'd be losers or winners in some timeless battle for significance. I care about things like that, but acknowledge that "winning and losing" are human notions, irrelevant against the backdrop of time. Cosmic significance is my little literary conceit, not the universe's. Note to self: just try to love and be loved, and hurt as few others as possible.

HORSES AND BUFFALO

*P*retty Shield told Frank Linderman a couple of stories about the role of horses in Crow life. Clans counted their wealth by their herds, and her village was a wealthy one. One time when they were moving, Pretty Shield's best friend was riding a horse which had always been gentle. This time, though, it went crazy and started to run. The girl fell off, but her foot caught in the harness. Her screams and dragging, flailing weight panicked the horse so that it ran harder than ever, bouncing her across rocks and through cactus beds.

By the time they stopped the horse, the girl was covered with blood and cactus spines. They carried her to a safe place, picked out spines, and bound her wounds. But she died in their arms. Pretty Shield grieved her friend's death for months.

She told another story about her father's best horse, which he rode on buffalo hunts and war parties. He doubly prized it because he had stolen it from the Lakota, which was a great coup. Out hunting, this horse seemed to know what its rider wanted and even what the buffalo was thinking.

One day, again while the village was being moved, he let Pretty Shield ride it to give it a little exercise. Pretty Shield and her friends ranged far from the moving village, talking, laughing, even stopping to play games. Wandering over the horizon, they came onto a herd of buffalo. To show off, she decided to try roping a calf. This ignited its inner fire for the hunt. It surged beneath her, galloped toward the calf at breakneck speed, and she had to hold on for dear life. She lost her nerve and dropped her rope.

Galloping amid the shaggy creatures, Pretty Shield began to scream. To her relief, she heard her father's voice. He had seen the girls ranging too far and followed them. Now he deftly rode between Pretty Shield and the running buffalo, skillfully "cutting" her from the surging herd.

Once they were safe, he laughed at her. "This horse has more sense than you do," he said. "He knew how to hunt, but all you knew how to do was scream." He never punished her, she told Linderman. The Great Plains Nations were gentle with their children. But he never let her ride his special horse again.

As a parent myself, decades ago, my heart was in my mouth because my four-year-old daughter took our dog for a walk around the block without telling me. Pretty Shield, her father, Plenty Coups—they all make me feel like a wimp. I understand life at the bottom of the sea about as well as their lives. Not that I understand my great-grandfather's life much better.

CROW BUTTE

$\mathcal{I}$ have a habit I picked up from my mother. As long ago as I can remember, watching a historical movie or some documentary, Mom would head for our well-thumbed encyclopedia set. "I want to know what *really* happened," she'd say. I still relish her fact-checking and context-setting.

Mom died just as the information age was gathering steam. She would really have fun now, with a laptop and web access. This age's richness of data would have dazzled and delighted her.

When we open ourselves to one another's stories, we join in a psychological, neurological way—a way I would call spiritual. I find more reverence in wonder and curiosity about one another than in any number of stained glass windows or recited prayers. On my rolling spiritual retreat, I found it natural to expand my exploration any evenings I stayed in a motel. Linderman's interviews, geological and paleontological information, all got funneled into a good search engine to form my evening's liturgy.

As I drove away from Fort Robinson, a sandstone prominence south of US Highway 20 caught my eye. It loomed pale and craggy, labeled on my map as Crow Butte. The same Crow Nation of Pretty Shield and Plenty Coups? I wondered. I knew my next web departure was scheduled.

That evening, the bright screen confirmed that it was. In the early 1800s, I read, the Crow and Lakota fought over this part of the plains. After the Lakota drove them west into Montana, the Crow would still return from time to time to seek vengeance.

One winter a Crow raiding party hit James Bordeaux's trading post, burned it, and made off with a hundred head of horses he was holding for the Lakota. Bordeaux's family escaped and took shelter with a Lakota Chief named Grabbing Bear. Because horse-stealing was a matter of tribal honor, Lakota warriors set off after the invaders.

When they caught up, a running battle ensued. The outnumbered Crow abandoned the stolen horses and retreated to the top of the butte that now bears their name. They couldn't escape, but neither could the Lakota climb up in the face of arrows and rocks hurled from above. So the Lakota besieged the place. For three nights, they could hear the Crow above them, singing and dancing in defiance. Sooner or later, the Lakota were certain, the Crow would run out of food and water. Then the singing and dancing would end. They would be made to pay.

On the fourth day, the Lakota heard nothing. Climbing the butte and investigating, they found the top of the mountain empty. One section of cliff had looked too precipitous to descend, so the Lakota had left it unwatched. Now, they found, the Crow had let themselves down on rawhide ropes and escaped. That's how Crow Butte got its name.

I find a moral in this story. Survivance. In the midst of singing and dancing their defiance, the Crow sought a pragmatic way to survive. They didn't get to keep the horses they had stolen. But even in returning home from the adventure, they achieved a victory of the spirit. Technological, Euro-American culture has something to learn from such stories.

We can sure pray that no one ever makes a Hollywood movie about us. Inspired by my visit to Fort Robinson, I later took time to re-watch John Ford's movie, *Cheyenne Autumn*. As a fourteen-year-old, I had considered his portrayal of the Cheyenne Exodus touching and profound. Watching it again, fifty years later, I decided some old memories are best left alone.

John Ford was a legendary director. Many of his movies are classics, still taught in film classes. He claimed he filmed *Cheyenne Autumn*, his final western, to make up for Holly-wood (himself as much as anybody) stereotyping Native Americans as evil, bloodthirsty savages.

I guess I should appreciate the attempt, but *Cheyenne Autumn* is ponderous, and mired in cliché and mid-twenti-eth-century racism. Ford was blind to stereotypes which now seem obvious, even creepy. Meanwhile, the most distressing violence committed by the Cheyenne, and upon them, is sanitized out of existence.

I read that the movie did, however, mark an important cultural moment. Just not for the reasons Ford intended. He was fond of shooting in Monument Valley on the Arizona-Utah border. That bore no resemblance to the settings where the real events took place, but the towering sandstone spires and sprawling red desert made spectacular backdrop. It also allowed Ford to draw from the local Navajo Reservation for extras and minor speaking roles.

Cheyenne Autumn features several scenes where the Cheyenne speak among themselves. They're not Cheyenne speaking Cheyenne, though, they're Navajos speaking Navajo. White director that Ford was, "Indians" were "Indi-ans" as far as he was concerned. No white audience would understand their words. So he told the Navajo extras just to ad lib while the cameras rolled. That was old Hollywood practice.

The movie lost money at the box office, but was a hit in Navajo communities. As it turns out, the Navajo actors took the occasion to indulge themselves in a tradition they had developed with Hollywood directors: talking dirty with a straight face.

They had learned to deal sly insults and out-and-out filth in a way that sounded like the dialogue the director wanted. In one scene of treaty negotiations, for example, they're actually carrying on a ribald conversation, graphic and hilarious, about the great director's penis size. All without cracking a ghost of a smile. As a western, the movie failed. But for Navajo audiences it was uproarious satire.

This ruthless mocking of Euro-American cultural stereotypes was, film scholars say, an important moment in indigenous self-identity. Survival + resistance = survivance. The very idea of survivance begins by accepting that the old way of life is gone forever. I would not have foreseen this: creatively adapting to that change can involve a defiant sense of humor.

In the Navajos' case, I lift my glass to salute the subversiveness that creative humor can express. May it level hierarchy and strengthen the heart in evil times. As long as a still-disadvantaged culture like the Navajo can make fun of the dominant culture, I see hope for all of us.

A MEDICINE DREAM

*T*he next night I read Plenty Coups again. Reading between the lines, I think he was being groomed for leadership even as a boy. In 1856 he was nine years old and the Lakota were pressing his people hard. Both his parents had been killed in Lakota raids. His older brother, whom he greatly admired, then went on a war party to seek revenge, and never returned.

Losing his family that way, Plenty Coups's heart "fell to the ground" as he describes it. He was too young to go on a war party, but still felt the weight of his village's fortunes on his shoulders. It was a time to wait, mourn, and dream.

Medicine dreams were, I read, essential to many First Nations, including the prairie hunters. Great leaders dreamed great dreams. To open the spirit to such dreaming, a person would go without food and drink, journey to a lonely place, even cut or sacrifice parts of one's own body as an offering.

Plenty Coups slipped away from his village, fasted for two days, then climbed a high butte. He pulled off his clothes, cleansed himself in smoke from burning herbs, then cut his arms to let the blood flow. Cleansed and empty, he built a mat of sweet sage, lay down, and slept.

He told Linderman how he woke to the sound of a voice calling his name. As he walked toward the voice, a mighty lodge rose up before him. The voice told him to go in. Old men sat in a circle inside, and he knew they were magical. On one side sat the Bad Storms, ugly faces that glared as they howled for him to go away. They embodied ill fortune for the Crow people. Then a kind voice on his right invited him to come sit on that side. These were Dwarfs, he told Linderman, magical Persons of great power. They give him a fistful of fine arrows and told him it was time to count coup.

Nine-year-old Plenty Coups had never been in battle, and could not count coup as a warrior. But as the Dwarfs jabbed one arrow after another into the ground, telling a story around each one, he realized they were counting coups he would attain in battles yet to come. That finally impressed even the Bad Storms, who consented that he could remain.

Reaching back through the years, Plenty Coups shared with Linderman his memory of their words. "The Creator has given you what you need. You must use the powers the Creator gave you." He understood this to mean his strength was not just physical. He needed to hone his senses and his wits. Some medicine dreams had to be interpreted by wise old leaders, Plenty Coups explained, but not this one. The Bad Storms would afflict the Crow. Mere strength would not be enough to save his people; he needed to use all his gifts.

PLENTY COUPS AND PRETTY SHIELD

I believe Plenty Coups's and Pretty Shield's stories have much to teach us today. I also bear in mind their stories are small pieces in a vast tapestry. More than five hundred First Nations blanketed the continent when Europeans first arrived. Each had its own richness of tradition.

I have read biographies of other indigenous leaders. My observation is that Euro-American writers tend to make their subjects props in the Euro-American story. I therefore appreciate that Linderman tried to keep Plenty Coups's and Pretty Shield's own voices. I appreciate the journey they take me on, and highly recommend both books.

Both begin as charming coming-of-age tales in a land that seems dauntingly violent and dangerous to my twenty first-century sensitivity. Always matter-of-fact, Plenty Coups tells gripping tales of hunting buffalo and wars against enemy Nations. Pretty Shield speaks more of Crow legendry and day-to-day life. Though their stories apparently didn't seem exotic to them, they peered keenly into the wonder beneath sod and sagebrush. Most striking to me, they accepted the human and organic nature that lay at the core of some of the most ghastly scenes.

Plenty Coups's contest with the buffalo, the death of Pretty Shield's friend, even Pretty Shield's misadventure with her father's hunting horse, stay with me. These were pre-teen children! The demands on children growing up in their world could be deadly serious, yet both lived with them and described them in a spirit of appreciative remembrance.

In one story, Pretty Shield, tells of playing with friends and finding a dead Lakota warrior. His people had left his body in an abandoned tipi, which was their funeral custom. The girls found the tipi, went in, and saw the dead man with a bullet hole in his forehead. Play-mimicking women's work after a battle, they stripped the body. Their parents rebuked them for that, but such child's play! All the same, Pretty Shield and Plenty Coups moved confidently and mostly happily through their world, at least to hear them tell it. Both told Linderman, "We had everything we needed." This was the world, the life they knew, and they were good with it.

Plenty Coups calls up images that remind me of medieval knighthood: proving oneself in battle was more important than victory. But the glitter and pageantry of European knighthood masked the savagery of medieval life. Knights routinely plundered, slaughtered civilians, or merely allowed them to starve. Plenty Coups describes horrific scenes of war between Crow and Lakota or Crow and Blackfeet. They rode their violent world with calm acceptance. Also worth mentioning in our time, they only measured their dead in half dozens, not thousands.

Many of their stories throb with a gorgeous naturalism. They sing matter-of-factly of poetic discourse with animals, winds, the land: advisors and helpers of human beings. Perhaps in a dangerous world, their magic and music were more than mere metaphor, but real psychic medicine. By age eight, every Crow boy or girl plainly knew what courage was, and honor, and what was expected of them. They knew to lean on natural forces that upheld and healed them.

My daily life is about grocery lists, central heat, motor transportation, processed food, the nearest web access. I find it sad, but hardly surprising, that my land-hungry Euro-American ancestors looked on indigenous peoples as a different species. Centuries would pass before Euro-American culture would even begin to recognize indigenous spirituality at any level. Such appreciation still dangles between dismissal on one side and romantic stereotype on the other.

By the 1880s settlers had overrun Montana. The government had put the Crow onto reservations, same as the Cheyenne and Lakota before them. Pretty Shield and Plenty Coups both express their devastation in the same way. "Our hearts fell on the ground and nothing happened after that. We are moving through a world we do not know."

As a Euro-American descendant myself, I mark that technological society can get so complicated, we don't understand it, either. There's a spirit to technological creation that seems to slip the tether and run ahead, out of sight of the very people who create it.

BISON ANTIQUUS

$\mathcal{M}$y little car threw up dust along a tooth-rattling, washboard road that crossed the same Nebraska badlands where Mike Voorhies had once dug up those two Columbian mammoths. Twenty bouncy miles later, I found myself at one more gravel parking lot. One more dirt path led down a hillside, this one to a small, Monet-like pond. Glassy water mirrored sky, cattails, willow, balm-of-Gilead. I walked across an earth fill dam. Before me was my destination, a long building shaped like a Quonset hut.

A thick, sandstone aquifer lies close to the surface here, a spring thousands of years old. It formed a marsh which, in the 1950s, two ranchers named Albert Meng and Bill Hudson decided to turn into a stock pond. As they cleared brush and bulldozed dirt, Meng discovered bones weathering out of the hillside.

For years, everyone thought they were just sheep bones. Damned big sheep bones, though. Hudson and Meng finally took samples to a nearby state college where an archaeologist, Larry Agenbroad, identified them as bison

REFLECTIONS

bones. Not just any bison bones, either, but from an extinct species, *Bison antiquus,* ancestor of the bison we know today. I reflect, as an atheist, that makes *Bison antiquus* one of those "transitional" fossils that creationists tell us don't exist.

Hundreds of them existed in this place. The Hudson-Meng Bison Kill site was a major discovery, a mass dying four hundred years after our two Columbian mammoths got themselves dead a few miles away in their alpha male battle.

Archaeologists are basically just garbage pickers who use the methods of crime- scene investigators. They analyze the leavings of bygone cultures to deduce how the people lived. Mixed in with the bison bones, Agenbroad found flint spear points, dart points, and knives. He also found burned and cracked bones, scarred from butchering.

This, he concluded, was the site of an ancient slaughter. "Paleoindians," anthropologist jargon for prehistoric First Nations, drove a bison herd over a cliff, finished them off, and butchered them. He estimated that about eighty Paleoindians dried enough meat here to feed them all winter. Early European explorers on the Great Plains later saw indigenous hunters still using this same technique. It's called a buffalo jump.

After cataloguing and analysis, they covered the bones back over to preserve them. Fifteen years later, two more archaeologists, Larry Todd and David Rapison, re-excavated the site and reached a different conclusion. They said the bones showed evidence of natural decay and chewing by scavengers. What's more, they concluded, the Paleoindian artifacts were not all the same age. The flint spear points were an early technology. Stone-tipped darts weren't invented till much later.

Therefore, they said, the human artifacts were deposited at the site through decades of on-and-off occupation. Todd

71

and Rapison didn't see any evidence of a prehistoric cliff for the bison to fall over in the first place. So no buffalo jump.

They therefore produced a different conclusion. The bison perished in some natural event, perhaps a range fire. The ancient marsh would have been a watering place for animals and humans alike. The artifacts were left by indigenous hunters who camped there, year after year, long after the bison died. Each visit would leave castoff tools and trash, which eventually filtered into the soil and got mixed in with the bones just by accident.

Long story short, it breaks down into three possibilities. The Paleoindians *might* have killed and butchered the bison. Or they *might* have come onto the dying or dead animals, finished them off, and eaten them. Or maybe they just happened to be in the neighborhood long after and got accused of the slaughter thousands of years later.

Scientists get into this kind of argument all the time. It's where a lot of the fun of science is. It will take more detective work to solve this mystery, if it ever does get solved. Meanwhile, displays at the site invited visitors to come up with our own theory on how the Paleoindians lived and how the bison died.

Walking through the warehouse-sized shelter built over the site, I could read the displays and peer into the archaeologists' trenches for myself. Hundreds of bones lay in a thick tangle at the bottom of the largest trench, jumbled together in a charnel testament to bygone ages. It brought back images of the Ashfall Fossil Site and also, in a way, those satellite images of forests knocked over by Mount St. Helens. We may be born and spend our lives striving to be individuals. But in death, we are a species.

Most fascinating for me were the display cases of stone-age artifacts from the site: spear points, smaller tips from spear-thrower darts, stone scrapers, long flint knives. Flint arrowheads had also been added for comparison. The bow and arrow were invented much later, a mere fifteen hundred years ago in North America.

I've handled stone arrowheads and flint knives. They're elegant, well-balanced tools. The pressure flaking technique produces a hard, sharp edge you don't want to mess with. They were crafted by people who really knew what they were doing. If I could operate a laptop as well as they operated a couple pieces of stone, I would be a happy man.

Studying the bones, I was also getting used to such massed evidence of death. I could begin to understand what Mike Voorhies told me. If you want to know what really went on ten thousand or one million years ago, a bone bed is not grisly. It's a rare and exciting window into a bygone world.

The world holds no more death than life, I reflect. You can't have one without the other. In the broad scope of things, a cemetery or site like this is a legacy, a celebration. I reflect that death's greatest purpose for the living may just be to make us pay attention. It's an inescapable demonstration that something bigger than us is going on.

"It is a good day to die," Crazy Horse was fond of saying before a battle. That's a paradox I admit I struggle to get my head around. I'm fine pondering distant stars, but reluctant to engage dead sparrows. I'd much rather work, play, watch a movie, mow a lawn, and pretend my road will go on, nicely paved, forever. I'm not as eager to think about what's happened throughout history to all those other temporary schmucks. And that I'm going to share that same fate.

Then I see a mass of bones like this. And woops, dang, death is still here. I, too, am temporary. Is it really a good day to die? I can't answer that question. But I suspect that sometime next week—or next year—or next decade—would be better.

But those ancient pieces of flint, the subtle crafting of them and the marks they made on bison bone so long ago: they, too, are real. People journeyed this way ten thousand years ago. They lived and loved, same as I do. They killed and carved and cooked and ate, same as I do (or pay others to do for me.) Same as my descendants will hopefully do generations hence.

They invented, hunted, and crafted their subtle marvels of stone. They fashioned lives out of materials with which we no longer have skills. They knew what they were doing and I bet they talked and laughed while they did it. I would love to hear the sound of a Paleoindian joke. And you can't have the barbecue without the bones.

So bring 'em on, those bones. If life is inevitable tragedy, let us celebrate that tragedy.

RED WOMAN'S BONES

$\mathcal{M}$y laptop cast a glow on my face. Having showered in my motel room, I was now reading about flint arrowheads. They can be found all across the northwest plains if you know where to look. But I also read that the Crow never used flint arrowheads. Such tools were by an older culture, long vanished from lands the Crow later roamed. Plenty Coups and Pretty Shield agree, the Crow used iron arrowheads bartered from white traders. Before that they used arrowheads made of bone. But never flint.

Plenty Coups and Pretty Shield both told stories about flint arrowheads, though. They both considered them mysterious, with mystic power which gets translated to the English word, "medicine."

At age eight, Pretty Shield was playing one day with her friends, upstream from their village. The girls had crafted root-diggers, an implement Crow women used to dig up edible tubers. Playing, they dug into the stream bank at the base of a cliff. Pretty Shield's root digger struck something hard. Digging around it, she found not rock, but bone.

Together the girls dug up a large skull. It looked to them like a human skull, but twice as large as a grown man's head. It had big teeth, which frightened them. One girl, Shows-the-Lizard, laughed at the skull. But Pretty Shield was fearful and ran back to the village to tell her father.

He returned with her, picked up the skull, and solemnly looked it over. Then he shooed the girls away. They watched from a distance as he brought out his medicine pipe, lit it, and sat for a long while, smoking, communing with the skull. He finally put the pipe away, took off his good buffalo robe, and gently wrapped the skull with it. He dug a hole with his knife and re-buried the bundle. Later, Pretty Shield told Linderman, her father said, "That skull is strong medicine."

Pretty Shield regularly interpreted found objects as "strong medicine." Shows-the-Lizard made fun of her for being afraid of the skull. But when they were grown, Pretty Shield told Linderman, Shows-the-Lizard's first baby was killed in an accident. Pretty Shield had a baby at the same time and it lived. Therefore, she said, she was right to be afraid.

She mused that it might be the skull of Red Woman. Red Woman was the first woman, a very powerful Person. I later read that in some Crow legends, Red Woman eats humans. Pretty Shield never mentioned that, only that she was evil.

Back before the Crow had horses, some brave warriors captured Red Woman with ropes, made a great fire, and tried to burn her up. The fire burned all Red Woman's flesh until only her bones were left, growing hotter and hotter. Then it started to rain. Each raindrop caused pieces of her bones, shaped like arrowheads, to shatter off. Thousands and thousands of them shattered and flew all across the land. Pretty Shield told Linderman, that's why people still keep finding those pieces of flint. Those are Red Woman's bones. When the girls dug the skull up, they also found burned wood buried near it. So perhaps, she told Linderman, it was Red Woman's skull.

She told other stories about Red Woman. One time the village men found a pile of red flints. Some were tiny, about the size of a thumbnail. Some were long and skinny. Perhaps these red flints also came from Red Woman.

Red Woman got away from that trap, according to Pretty Shield. Some people say she was drowned later on. Others say she's still alive. It's all a mystery. The land is full of such mysteries, everywhere you go.

THE GHOST DANCERS

*E*ven after reams of reading and hours of talking (and listening) to people, I've only scratched the surface of First Nation life. Then again, after similar reams and hours, I can't say I understand the experience of my own ancestors in Ireland much better. I couldn't write in depth about either one.

I'm a product of Euro-American culture. I like to think I see into technological society. But the culture of my ancestors four generations back? Only as stories. North American culture here before my ancestors came? Only as stories. I do, however, know one thing for absolutely certain. For four hundred years, with distressing regularity, Euro-American culture practiced ruthlessness and called it virtue.

Acknowledging this, it wouldn't have been right to leave that corner of Nebraska without crossing into South Dakota to pay my respects at Wounded Knee. As students of American history know, the Wounded Knee Massacre marked the end of the so-called Indian Wars, the final, crushing blow on the Great Plains and, symbolically, the rest of the continent. Before Wounded Knee, suppression of indigenous peoples was about physical fighting. Afterward, it was what I'd call a more spiritual conflict: squeezing out the very sense the surviving First Nations had of themselves.

Decade by decade, dominant culture re-interpreted "the Indian" into stereotypes to be comfortably manipulated. By the twentieth century, Euro-American cultural assumptions of self, land, society, or who God was—or who God really loved—went unchallenged. It would not be unreasonable to say that spiritual war still goes on. Indigenous survivors still struggle, and have not forgotten who they are. As nearly as I can deduce, that's precisely what survivance is.

Located on what's now Pine Ridge Reservation, Wounded Knee was an atrocity born of misperception, paranoia, and finally, execution. Euro-Americans had spent centuries preaching to make indigenous peoples into "good Christians." But European and Native cultures were so different, how could anyone have expected a direct translation? Christianity thrives around the world precisely because it adapts so well and variously to different cultures.

In 1889, a Piute holy man in Nevada, named Wovoka, prophesied that if, for three years (the length of Jesus's ministry in Judea), First Nations gave up war, loved one another, lived righteous lives, and danced a variation on a familiar indigenous circle dance, Jesus would come to them. The wild game would return, white people would disappear, and they would live in peace and prosperity. The dance was called the Ghost Dance, but it was really a First Nations take on Christianity. Among indigenous cultures, what else would Jesus's "Kingdom of Heaven" look like?

The Ghost Dance movement swept through the reservations. By December 1890, the Lakota were practicing it heavily. Up at Standing Rock Reservation, the great Lakota chief, Sitting Bull, did not personally believe such white-inspired faith would do his people much good. But neither did he oppose the dances.

The growing movement made the US Army nervous as hell, though. Despite Sitting Bull's ambivalence toward the movement, the Indian Agent at Standing Rock blamed him. The agent ordered Sitting Bull's arrest in the dead of winter, which led to the chief being shot and killed by a reservation guard.

Amid growing tension, soldiers detained three hundred fifty Lakota villagers—for wanting peace and dancing. So deep was the army's fear of the villagers' intentions and capacities, it would make me laugh to keep from crying. Except that it doesn't. The paranoid folks had four hundred rifles, plus horse-drawn artillery. No, it doesn't make me laugh. Tears are the only appropriate response.

For the Lakota people, the massacre marks the tipping point between the genocide that came before and the attempted spiritual extermination that followed. For me, descendent of settlers that I am, I approached it as a place to humbly pay respects, reflect, and grieve the human condition.

WOUNDED KNEE

*T*he plains lay quiet beneath late September's sun as I navigated my way across Pine Ridge Reservation. It took some exploring to find the site. This being the off-season, no one was around as I stopped and got out of my car.

It felt odd to visit a place I'd read so much about. There was no Greek chorus or Wagner overture, just an occasional whistle from a shrike, impaling captured insects along a nearby barbed wire fence. A mild September breeze kissed my face. I gazed up at the low hill where the army stationed their Hotchkiss guns one hundred thirty years ago. A monument up there marks the mass grave where almost three hundred victims now lie buried.

Down on the flat right in front of me was where the Lakota set up their tipis. The lodges formed a long crescent, north to south. The Hotchkiss guns were aimed to cover the length of that camp. All I now saw were rough wooden booths along the parking lot, where Lakota craftspeople could sell their wares at the height of tourist season.

In 1890, Hotchkiss "mountain guns" were the latest technology, imported from France. Trained gunners could fire fifteen canisters a minute, each canister full of lead pellets the size of ball bearings. I do the math. Four Hotchkiss guns meant an explosion every second, lead shot blasting through a camp of mostly women and children. Meanwhile, the four hundred soldiers who surrounded the camp were also shooting at fleeing Lakota as fast as they could fire, reload, then fire again.

Three hundred Lakota and twenty-five soldiers died that day. Most of the army casualties were "friendly fire," bluecoats hitting other bluecoats in their own hysterical crossfire. This wasn't a military action. I'm not sure what word would contain it.

My shoes ground in gravel as I turned away and paced the road along a shallow gully which led down to Wounded Knee Creek itself. On that terrible day, terrified men, women, and children ran toward that gully, fell, then crawled in chaos through brush and snow. The only shelter from the relentless gunfire, the gully was no shelter at all. I studied the sparse trees and brush and pictured wood splintering in the hail of bullets. You have to know the story of a place to appreciate its spirituality. Knowing the story, my sense of this place was heartrending.

This all happened just a few days after Christmas. It was not a good day to die. The weather was so cold the dead, even the merely wounded, froze solid before they could be moved. Because of the frozen ground, the dead lay in the snow for days before the dirt could be chiseled down far enough to bury them.

I sat there for a long time, pondering and reflecting. My eyes swept the flat horizon, from the low hill north of me to the gully where so many huddled. My mind conjured women screaming, children screaming in terror, soldiers shouting orders, guns, explosions crashing together, insane thunder that still echoes over the generations. When the firing finally stops, my mind hears crying and whimpering from the wounded and terrified. That doesn't last long in the bitter cold. A few last rifle shots echo as soldiers chase those survivors still able to run away. Later, I learned, the US government would issue twenty (count 'em) twenty Congressional Medals of Honor to soldiers involved in this fiasco. What were we trying to tell ourselves? I wonder.

It was peaceful, that lovely fall day when I visited Wounded Knee. I struggled to reconcile clashing images of life, death, and tragedy, to hold in my mind that a cemetery is not just a remembrance but a celebration, and that in the really big picture, tragedy itself is a celebration. But this was a celebration cut brutally short. Might we learn something that we can use? Such violent heedlessness has to be marked. We need memorials. You'd never know something happened here if not for the markers.

Researching a writing project years back, I toured a beef slaughterhouse. Cattle were herded, single file, into a chute. One by one, they were driven into a narrow chamber where a man would reach out with what's called a bolt gun. Place it up to the cow's head, pull the trigger, pow! A plunger drives through bone and into the brain. Down goes the cow, hooks pick it up, hang it on an overhead conveyer, and away it trundles while the next customer walks in.

Bled out, skin taken off, insides taken out, the cow is disassembled in mere minutes. Parts whisk off in every direction for all kinds of different uses. It's just a business. The sides of beef are hanging in the cold room before the cow's body cells even know they're dead. Steaks, hamburger, hot dogs, cat food, fertilizer, even blood for medical research. Everything goes somewhere to get used by somebody.

For the employees on the scene, it was just business, another day at the office. Same thing at grocery stores that sell the beef. Same thing for the customers who buy steaks for barbecuing, hamburger for grilling, dog food for Fido. But the thing that stayed with me after that tour was the smell of the blood. It got into my head, lingered, took days to go away.

I finally did put the blood smell behind me. Sitting there at Wounded Knee, I had to wonder how long it would take for that heartbreak, and all it symbolizes, to go away. It's still with me as I write these words.

Given my modern, Euro-American sensibilities, I found the method by which the Crow killed buffalo, an arrow down through the abdomen, violent and cruel. I understand the "why" for it, after all, they had to shoot an arrow where it would penetrate. Plenty Coups's rite of passage, provoking the dying animal, could also be seen as cruel, both to the buffalo and to the child.

Modern slaughterhouses are, meat producers say, fast, efficient, and humane. They're hell for numbers, though. By the same token, I can look back at indigenous life on the plains and regard it as cruel, even nasty, brutish, and short. At the same time, in five short years of the Civil War, Euro-Americans patriotically killed far more of each other than all the First Nations who even lived on the Great Plains, put together. I don't know what to do with such comparisons.

Okay, death is a business. We all take part. We're all carbon-based life forms; we survive by chomping other carbon-based life forms. We all have skin in this game, one way or another. But what kind of business are we talking about, where can we draw a line between business and atrocity, struggling to survive versus inflicting horror and death just out of blind cussedness? How hard is it for the perpetrators of atrocity to tell the difference? These things mystify me.

A hundred years after I die, I won't care what killed me.

But for the sake of our own humanity, why in the moment is it so hard for conscience to assess the grade of death? Why is it so easy for people—any of us—to blast other human beings, whether or not they're trying to blast us?

They shot women and children with cannons? Really? I've heard sociologists counsel that this is what happens when an industrialized culture meets a hunter-gatherer culture. But that's unnerving in itself. Genocide is predictable—*only if human beings have no more free will than mosquitoes or microbes*. I would like to hope we're smarter than that. Sadly, the jury remains out.

Here's what chills me most. Suppose I could go back in time and ask General Sheridan, commander of the US Army in the "Indian Wars," or Colonel Forsyth, who commanded the soldiers at Wounded Knee, "Why did you do this heedless, terrible thing?" What chills me is that they might just say, "Are you kidding? We did it for you."

They did it for me. That's where the gig goes in. For me. For my great-grandfather, who had already given up on Nebraska by that time and trekked with his wife and surviving children back to eastern Iowa. Back in Iowa, though, they still farmed land from which the Santee and Fox and Chippewa had already been driven. It was done for me. I eat corn, wheat, and soybeans grown on land where indigenous men hunted buffalo and women scraped the hides, dried the meat, stitched the tipis, and sewed the moccasins. I partake in an economy that sprouts from ground fertilized by their blood. That's the shadow at the root of any spirituality I proclaim. However high I might reach in aspiration, roots below my feet, my roots, wind deeply into bloody soil. That's humbling. That is the humanity that reminds me how important perspective and patience and ideals are.

Whatever we believe in terms of religion, people follow careless gods. In the face of human nature, the best ethics we can manage are as reliably fickle as the wind. All I need to do is read any day's political news and I see it all over again.

Here's what the *Bismarck Tribune* opined as General Philip Sheridan's Army was pushing the Lakota off their land: "The Indian disappears before the advances of the white man . . . . The American[!] people need the land the Indians now occupy; many of our people are out of employment; the masses need some new excitement."

That paragraph perfectly expresses what Euro-Americans were calling "Manifest Destiny." Indigenous people were just the "old guard," so to speak, whom Euro-Americans had no choice but to eliminate in the name of progress.

I have my doubts. The next century is going to be an interesting ride. I see technology changing the world around us faster than we can adapt. In commerce and international relations, I wonder how long a center can hold.

Here's a question: just suppose indigenous peoples were not, as the *Bismarck Tribune* suggested, some old guard, who needed to be driven off the land and replaced for efficiency's sake. *Suppose they were just the advance guard*: exemplars of the cultural devastation we of consumer culture will bring upon ourselves as technology outstrips our ability to manage it?

What if the cyber-industrial culture in which I comfortably move cannot contain materialistic urges and cultural paranoia any better than Euro-American forbears contained their lust for land? What if the price of carbon-burning consumerism is to *follow* the "Indians" into diminished existence at best—or death at worst—shorn of resources and practices now taken for granted? In short: *how long do we have, and what will we do, when the Native American past becomes the Euro-American future?*

This party's not going to last forever. What if civilizations have lifespans, just as do individuals? What will that mean to Euro-American civilization? The jury's still out on that one, too. I wonder if we may someday learn, Euro-Americans didn't have so very much to teach Native Americans? And that First Nations' stories might have a great deal to teach, even now? The more I consider Plenty Coups's and Pretty Shield's lives, the more deeply I find myself pondering such questions.

PART III
STRONG MEDICINE

Knowledge is sorrow, but hope lies with the wisdom to live and love.
—Marty Two Bulls Sr, *Indian Country Today* magazine

URANIUM

 *N*avigating my way from Wounded Knee, I was still on Pine Ridge Reservation when I pulled to a stop at a T-intersection. Someone had nailed a weathered strip of plywood between two fence posts straight ahead of me. Hand painted letters cried, "NRC URANIUM EXPANSION HEARING . . . STOP the GENOCIDE & ECOCIDE NOW! #SHUT DOWN CROW BUTTE." Smaller print gave date and time for a public hearing.

Was this, I wondered, the same Crow Butte where Lakota battled Crow one hundred fifty years ago? My next motel night brought a web search which revealed, sure enough, it was. Crow Butte is now leased by a company called Crow Butte Nuclear Resources. They mine uranium from far beneath those beetling boulders where indigenous warriors once battled one another. Crow Butte Nuclear Resources had applied to the Nuclear Regulatory Commission for a license to expand. That was the reason for the hearing the sign announced.

Nuclear energy is strong medicine of a sort no one foresaw in Plenty Coups's or Pretty Shield's heyday. I hadn't connected it to this prairie either, till now. But in 1980, geologists discovered that an ancient layer of ash from western volcanoes, deposits now far underground, contained enough uranium to exploit commercially.

Crow Butte Nuclear Resources uses a method called "in-situ recovery." They drill hundreds of feet down, then use high pressure pumps to inject water laced with baking soda into the surrounding stone. The soda leaches out the uranium compounds. The uranium-rich water is then pumped up a separate well and refined into what's called yellowcake. That's the stuff the US government accused Saddam Hussein of buying as part of their excuse for invading Iraq in 2003.

Crow Butte ships several hundred tons of yellowcake a year to their parent company, Cameco, headquartered in Saskatoon, Canada. Owned mostly by Canadian federal and provincial governments, Cameco is the largest uranium producer in the world. They sell as far away as India and China. Crow Butte is actually one of their smaller holdings.

My web search took me deep into the story behind that plywood sign. As world economic development demands more energy, uranium becomes an increasingly hot (so to speak) commodity. Hence, Crow Butte's request to expand their operation.

That concerns some Lakota on Pine Ridge Reservation. Radioactive waste hangs around a very long time. Some wastewater winds up in evaporation ponds, but most is pumped down yet a third series of wells to be stored in deep rock layers below the water table. It's not exactly fracking, but similar technology.

Other byproducts from the refining process include radioactive dust and radon gas on the surface. But this NRC hearing, I learned, was mostly to field concerns about underground pollution in the aquifer itself.

We are tied to our planet by interlocked systems which spiral through time: the water we drink, the food we eat, the air we breathe, the waste we produce, our own bodies. We are sustained by nature's networks, complex and subtle. I wonder if, in their poetic way, the Crow and Lakota didn't understand this better than today's consumer culture does. Western spirituality, acknowledged or not, centers on domination of natural processes rather than relationship with them. But those relationships do exist. They don't always respond the way people expect them to.

For example, I learned about a spectacular underground water network called the Ogallala Aquifer. The Ogallala Aquifer is a massive water table that extends from Pine Ridge Reservation down through western Nebraska, Kansas, and Oklahoma, all the way south to the Texas panhandle. It's one of the largest underground water sources in the world, and Crow Butte sits right on top of it.

That would have amazed my great-grandfather. Back in the 1880s, Tom and Sarah McCarty went bust because they couldn't figure out how to raise crops with the meagre rainfall on the Nebraska plains. Other settlers did no better. Ironically, their dusty furrows lay only yards above a fresh water sea a thousand miles long.

If you fly over that same stretch of prairie nowadays, it's quilted green with lush circles and squares of cash crops. Time and technology bring us high pressure sprinkler irrigation, pumped up from the Ogallala Aquifer. That technology comes with fine print, though. This vast reservoir is a one-time resource. In two generations, it's been drawn down more than one hundred feet in some places. And population, technology, and water use accelerate each year, like a train rolling down a grade without brakes.

I reflect on this paradox. Technology increases like a breeder reaction, at a rate that takes by surprise even those who create it. Today's culture prospers by growing, buying, selling, and producing items our forbears never even imagined. But resources get depleted. Adverse effects crop up unexpectedly. Technological cleverness rebounds in ways we don't want, but can't foresee. So far, it's relatively easy to ignore the depletion of the Ogallala Aquifer. People just drill deeper and buy more pipe.

Going back to Crow Butte, citizen concern on Pine Ridge Reservation centered on the water itself. Not only was Crow Butte Nuclear Resources using large amounts of water, they were also exposing the aquifer to radioactive waste.

The NRC hearing had come and gone by the time I read about it. Crow Butte's people assured everyone that things were well in hand. Radioactive dust is carefully suppressed, they said. Radioactive wastewater is stored in impermeable layers far below the aquifer. Water pressure techniques, they said, keep it from going anywhere within the aquifer itself. The dropping level has little to do with their activities. They're being model citizens and good job creators.

I don't have a snappy comeback to all that. I do sympathize with the Lakota at the hearing, who spoke of water not just as a cash account to be drained, but as a living entity to which, like all living entities, we are connected.

I'd be lying if I denied my appreciation for the comforts advanced technology provides. But it's always a paradox—innovation rises in human nature like any other drive. But we are continually relearning; we can't even control ourselves, let alone the inventions we create. I worry that we're clever enough to find our grandchildren facing a hell we blithely created for them without realizing it.

Take, for example, a place called Optima Lake. In 1950 the Army Corps of Engineers set out to fix a dual problem in Oklahoma, the southern end of the Ogallala Aquifer. Each year, spring rains would bring damaging floods along Beaver

Creek. Then by summer, the rain would cease, the land would grow dry, and crops would go thirsty. The solution seemed simple. Build a reservoir. It would restrain the spring floods, then provide water for irrigation through the summer. Meanwhile, people could boat, swim, water ski, and fish in the new lake. What's not to like?Alas, before the Army Corps of Engineers' bulldozers even finished pushing dirt, crop irrigation pumped up from the Ogallala Aquifer lowered the local water table. A century ago, the aquifer fed Beaver Creek and the Platte River. Then the falling levels caused those springs to fail. By the end of the 1970s, even as Optima Lake was being completed, Beaver Creek had dried up almost completely.

So by the time Optima Lake was finished, there were no more floods to control, nor was there even a stream to feed it. Even in the wet season, there's only a puddle where Beaver Creek trickles across the bottom of the empty reservoir.

The Army Corps of Engineers' website sums it up best—it would be hilarious, except that it's not. "Visitors should be aware that the lake's level . . . may offer no water-based recreation and may not be suitable for swimming, fishing, boating, or other activities. Visitors should come for the quiet natural setting—with or without water in the lake area."

Vested in the human condition, I can't think of a better paradox to sum up our high tech, postmodern way of life: a brand new "lake" too dry to swim in.

In reflective moments, though, my own heart, Euro-American though it is, senses and reverberates to earth's interwoven complexity. Such "medicine," to use Pretty Shield's term, is beyond easy reduction. A culture that exploits natural resources finds itself nipped in the butt by ingenuity that's larger than its foresight. We can now grow soybeans on fields that defeated my great-grandfather's best efforts. But the floods that once rolled down Beaver Creek now soak invisibly into the thirsty ground.

Generations ago, Euro-Americans exterminated the buffalo and insisted the "Indians" take up farming, mind you, on the same kind of land that defeated my great- grandfather. Now there's deep well irrigation. But on Pine Ridge Reservation north of Crow Butte, should it be surprising that Lakota worry about dropping water tables and pollution from uranium mining?

A year after I read about Optima Lake, the Dakota Access Pipeline controversy swept across North Dakota's Standing Rock Reservation. That involved many of the same concerns. Also much the same response from government and commercial interests. History is a parallel symphony of resonant chords. If the Lakota feel as though their genocide continues into the twenty-first century, I can't blame them.

A century and a half after Crow and Lakota warriors battled there, Crow Butte still holds troubled energy. But the trouble isn't in the land. It's in the people.

On the other hand, one thing the Dakota Access Pipeline controversy made manifest is that the US government can no longer play First Nations off one another the way the army did in the 1870s. They long ago caught on to that strategy. They presented a unified front in North Dakota. Part of survivance, I conclude, is learning who your allies are and who your real opponents are.

The vision that sticks with me is that well pipe below Crow Butte, throbbing with the gritty swill of uranium mining on the high plains. Down and down the wastewater pumps, through the Ogallala Aquifer, past layers where *Bison Antiquus* and Columbian mammoths roamed, through the layer of deadly ash spewed by the super volcano that buried all those short-legged rhinos. Ever deeper, past ever more ancient stone and fossils, to be stored in (of all places, Crow

Butte's literature tells us) the Morrison Formation, famous farther west for its Jurassic dinosaur fossils.

We drill through the immensity of age with our diamond-studded bits. Two hundred years ago we neither dreamed of such tools, nor the need for them. We didn't dream of nuclear reactors, either, or such creatures as *Diplodocus* or *Allosaurus*. Now we flood their bones with our radioactive shit. That's creativity for you. Is Red Woman laughing at us?

When a buyer from the other side of the world purchases oil from North Dakota oil shale or yellowcake from beneath Crow Butte, is there any reverence? Does anyone take a moment to wonder at the hugeness of what they're doing, or the hugeness of what we touch that we don't fully understand? Or is it just about the money, sign on the dotted line and deposit the check?

To put it more poetically, when Pretty Shield and her friends found that skull buried in the prairie loam, her father honored it for the mystery it represented. Lots of things lie buried in the earth, old bones and old isotopes. Just my prejudice, maybe, but it seems to me it couldn't hurt to sit and smoke with all of them for a good, long time before people hustle off to sell them.

Pretty Shield's father lived a life as different as it could be from mine. That was the old spirit, as the *Bismarck Tribune* proclaimed, versus the "new" Euro-American spirit. But I love what he did. We could learn something there, or at least I think I learned something from reading about him.

Attendance, I read, was sparse at that NRC hearing in Nebraska. The Nuclear Regulatory Commission representatives seemed to go out of their way to be perceived as listening to all voices. But there weren't many voices. I'm not surprised that Crow Butte Nuclear Resources received their license to expand.

Oil fields blossom in North Dakota. The center-pivot

sprinklers in Kansas and Oklahoma continue to spray. Optima Lake stays dry. Yellowcake circulates around the world, powering nuclear icebreakers in Russia and electrical generating stations in China. Meanwhile the fine print waits. We will only notice it later.

Innovation has become a living thing. It may not exactly be *larger* than the humanity that produces it, but it is certainly *faster*. We labor mightily on our inventions, then scramble to chase them down roads we never dreamed they'd take. The lives of my grandchildren will be more different from my life, than mine is from that of my great-grandparents. I can only hope they'll be better. But creativity does not guarantee this.

MINUTEMAN

*E*uro-American culture thought it was a great thing to draw water up from the Ogallala Aquifer. Likewise, when Enrico Fermi and his team of physicists produced the first nuclear reaction, we spent the next three decades celebrating that. I've been to the memorial that now marks their experimental atomic pile. It was set up beneath the stands of the University of Chicago's football stadium, but there's no stadium there anymore. Just a plaza with a striking sculpture by Henry Moore.

Moore's piece is way nicer than anything at Wounded Knee. At the same time, its vaguely mushroom shape conveys real ambivalence about Fermi's accomplishment. By the late 1960s when the piece was commissioned, nuclear power had evolved in ways Fermi and his colleagues had not foreseen.

I've likewise visited Los Alamos, New Mexico, where hundreds of physicists worked together to create the first atom bombs. Like Fermi's team, those scientists also thought they were working for the good, rushing to develop nuclear weapons before Hitler's scientists could beat them to it.

After we dropped two of those bombs on Japan, though,

second thoughts gradually emerged like maggots on a corpse. Maggots are, I reflect, a necessary piece of biological process. They're nasty in the moment, but in the grand scheme of things, they break down death and make way for new life. Too-late second thoughts about atomic weaponry have a more complex role. Creativity seems all for the good in the excitement of the moment. In the long run, though, is rarely either bad nor good in itself. It makes life exponentially more complicated, exponentially faster than we expect.

Now I was driving west on Interstate 90, a couple hours north from Pine Ridge Reservation. Cars and huge tractor trailer rigs screamed past me. No one seemed to notice the low, fenced compounds here and there along the right-of-way. I wouldn't either, except one was my next stop. A brochure spread out beside me indicated the next freeway exit. A frontage road led to a nondescript quadrangle. Eight-foot chain link fence guarded a single-story, cream-yellow building.

Other tourists pulled in, one by one. A sign on the locked gate read, "Delta 01 Launch Control Facility. Restricted area." A military-looking, green armored car sat inside the fence. Beyond that, another sign warned people to keep away from a knee-high concrete cone. It was a high frequency radio antenna, it said, hardened to withstand a nuclear blast. Thinking back to Fermi and those physicists at Los Alamos, I again reflected how innovation and human nature can build momentum, speeding ahead of expectations until we have to run to catch up.

Freeway traffic whined a quarter mile away. In the distance, a combine worked its way slowly across a field, harvesting and thrashing the golden wheat. All around us stretched the middle of Middle America.

We tourists talked and joked about the armored car, the blast-proof electronic circuitry, and the low building before us with the most blah-looking aluminum siding you ever saw. It would have been boringly nondescript if not for the searchlights, radio antennae, cameras, and motion detectors all over it.

A National Park Service truck pulled in and a young man got out. He wore a Park Service uniform and "Smoky Bear" hat. We shook hands all around, then he unlocked the gate. "Welcome to the Minuteman Missile National Historic Site," he said. "You are about to enter a war zone."

This was one of two missile memorials to honor a key weapon in the so-called cold war between the United States and the Soviet Union. The other was one state north, in North Dakota. A generation ago, Minuteman missile sites covered thousands of square miles of America's heartland. Some are still active.

You can, I found out, spend dozens of hours poring over online articles and old training videos on the nuclear arms race. For forty years, it sucked up the cream of innovation in the United States and Soviet Union. The name of the game, they said, was not to conquer, but to counter "nuclear aggression" by the foe, by delivering a crushing "response." We raced to build bigger nuclear warheads, better ways to protect them, and more efficient ways to deliver them. So as to kill lots of "bad guys." The bad guys were "them," not "us." I have no doubt "they" said the same thing about "us."

For a generation, the two most powerful nations in the history of the world displayed the same kind of paranoia the US Army showed at Wounded Knee. This quiet stretch of prairie was ground zero. In five years, from 1958 to 1963, the United States designed and installed one thousand hardened steel-and-concrete underground missile silos beneath the plains. We built indestructible (we hoped) underground command centers and security systems. One hundred nondescript one-story buildings, one hundred chain link compounds, one hundred armored cars for security patrol, thousands of miles of underground wiring to launch all those missiles on five minutes' notice. Each missile in its silo was the most compact, deadly engine of war human ingenuity could then devise.

All those missile silos still comprised a mere third of our overall "deterrent." Submarines off our coasts also bristled with nuclear missiles. Sprawling air bases could launch additional squadrons of nuclear-armed jet bombers. This was, in defense analysts' terms, our nuclear "triad." The Soviet Union was doing the same thing. Other nations also joined in.

Experts coined the term "overkill," to express each nation's capacity to destroy the other many times over. The famous theory was that the peace had to hold, because if either nation started a war, both were sure to be destroyed. "Mutual Assured Destruction" it was called, appropriately shortened to MAD. The craziest thing about MAD is that for more than a generation it seems to have worked.

The United States and Russia finally reined in the nuclear arms race a bit, not from reason, but expense. Those damned warheads and missiles could bankrupt a nation. In the late twentieth century, they reduced warheads by about half. Of course there are still more than enough to blow each other to smithereens. Meanwhile, smaller powers continue to join the club. North Korea, for example.

So here I was, waiting for the National Park Service tour through this deactivated control center. Other cut-back sites were destroyed as part of Strategic Arms Reduction Treaties. The land was sold back to the farmers from whom the military had procured it before the whole paranoid business began. (The indigenous people, who hunted buffalo across this prairie before the farmers came, had been gone so long, it didn't occur to anyone to give the land back to them.)

The ranger led us around this control site, exuberantly

describing the Minuteman program and its capabilities. Such a quiet scene now. This one center, on five minutes' notice, was designed to wipe ten or more different cities off the face of the earth!

He unlocked the building and we followed him in. We peeked through doorways at sleeping quarters, an entertainment center with all the amenities for the soldiers who guarded the complex and its ten missile silos. They did regular patrols in the green armored car. Between patrols, if a motion sensor picked up movement at a silo site, armed guards would scramble to investigate. If you happened to be wandering around the chain link perimeter at a silo, you'd be in big trouble. So, he told us with a smile, would a jackrabbit that was just trying to dig its way under the fence.

Off the hallway, he keyed a code into an electronically locked door. The latch clicked and he swung it open to reveal a cramped elevator. (The tour size, I later learned, was limited to the number of people who could squeeze into the elevator.) Down we rode, four stories into the earth, to a concrete corridor. A hand-painted mural on the concrete wall showed a Minuteman missile tearing through a Soviet flag. Another mural was painted on the four-foot-thick steel door into the launch control center itself. This one depicted a pizza box. Above, in stenciled letters: "WORLD-WIDE DELIVERY IN 30 MINUTES OR LESS." And below: "OR YOUR NEXT ONE IS FREE."

The guide ducked so his hat brim would clear the steel doorway into a Tylenol-shaped vault. We followed him into a tiny world of 1960s-era electronic equipment, indicator lights and rocker switches on all sides. Even as missiles and equipment were upgraded over the decades, he explained, they kept the old, hand-soldered circuitry. It was more robust than newer, printed circuits. Better able to withstand a nearby nuclear blast.

There were two identical control panels. Two officers at a time, called "missileers," would rotate through watches in this vault, twenty-four hours on, twenty-four hours off. A sequence of top secret pass codes admitted them to the elevator, unlocked the steel door to the vault, and also opened the red box with the missile launch keys.

Now that this site was decommissioned, the red box was no longer locked. He swung it open and showed us a folded manila envelope. It contained the confirmation codes, along with the two launch keys. They looked like any padlock keys.

He inserted a key into one of two launch switches, spaced twelve feet apart. To launch missiles, he said, both operators had to turn their keys at the same time. That way, it was impossible for a single operator to make a launch.

One tourist in a camouflage vest nudged his son, a dark-haired boy who looked about ten years old. "Why don't you turn that key and see what happens?" he said. The boy didn't respond. Even decommissioned, the console stared down bad jokes.

"One push of the button and a shot the world wide," folksinger Bob Dylan piped at the height of the cold war. "And you don't ask questions with God on our side." This would be the same God worshipped by Colonel Forsyth, commander of the troops at Wounded Knee? The same God worshipped by Fort Robinson's commander, Captain Wessels, when the Northern Cheyenne were being starved into submission?

In this missile control center, no, there would be no questions. "You were just trained to do it," a former missileer said on one online video I later watched. "We assumed that if we ever got orders, the Soviet missiles were already on their way."

Immense though the responsibility was, these two

missileers were just junior officers, near the bottom of the military totem pole. Orders and protocols filtered to them through a complex bureaucracy, all the way down from the White House. Failsafe on top of failsafe. At least that's how the system was designed to work.

I don't know what could possibly go wrong. First generation computers, thousands of miles of underground wiring, thousands of warheads, thousands of human beings keeping it all primed and ready. We're still here. I guess it worked well enough.

Well enough. But even deactivated, an oppressive spirit of foreboding lingered in that steel capsule.

THE WASHITA

*W*hile cyber-surfing and reflecting after my rolling spiritual retreat, I found myself deeply engaging the career of a historic, also legendary, Euro-American. To me, his life contained and was contained by spiritual tensions that still linger. I think he's best introduced on the dry prairie above the south end of the Ogallala Aquifer. That's where a narrow stream called the Washita River flows into what's now the state of Oklahoma.

It's the morning of November 26, 1868, not quite dawn, blisteringly cold. A line of Cheyenne and Kiowa villages stand for miles along the ice-crusted waters. Wisps of smoke rise from still-smoldering lodge fires. Gentle snores sound from some tipis. We're about to start that war the Bismarck Tribune called for.

Around the easternmost village, the US 7th Cavalry moves into position. Horse soldiers ease their way across the moonlit snow. They will attack at sunrise. No one speaks. Their breaths billow in soft jets. To get a little warmth, some men lean forward, against their horses' necks. That doesn't stop the shivering. They're not allowed to dismount and stamp their feet to keep warm. The sound might give them away.

This is how badly their commanding officer wants silence. He loves dogs. He owns many and takes them everywhere he goes, including on this campaign. But as they approached this village earlier, to make sure absolute silence was maintained, he ordered that the dogs be silenced with ropes and stabbed to death with sabers. Dogs might bark. The officer's name is George Armstrong Custer.

Now the sun's rays shoot red from the horizon. Bare tree branches cast their first, naked shadows as the bugler sounds the regimental call, "Gerryowen." The men charge in, shouting and shooting. A sleepy warrior named Double Wolf rushes from his tipi and fires a rifle. He misses and is the first to die in the hail of army bullets. Men and women tumble out of their furs, stagger from tipis, and run shouting and screaming. They try to hide in gullies or flee, splashing down the icy river. Soldiers ride after them, gunning them down as if on some kind of crazy hunt.

Black Kettle, the sixty-seven-year-old Cheyenne Chief, has always kept the peace. He has an old American flag an Indian agent once gave him, along with a promise that so long as the flag flew over their tipi, the Great White Father would protect them. He already knows the flag is useless. Four years earlier, the good citizens of Denver City raided his camp on the banks of Sand Creek in eastern Colorado. He and many villagers had huddled under that flag back then. It only made them better targets.

Now it's all happening again. Black Kettle runs from his tipi and manages to catch a pony amid the chaos. Old and stiff though he is, he vaults onto its back, grabs its mane, and rides back to his tipi. His wife, Medicine-Woman-Later, staggers out. He grabs her by the arm and hauls her up in front of him.

Their pony's hooves send water flying as they gallop across the river. A bullet strikes him in the back. He falls with a cry and Medicine-Woman-Later topples off with him. They land together in the frigid water. She tries to drag him to the bank, but he's too heavy. A bullet strikes the back of her head and she falls across him. Their blood mingles in cloudy streams, trailing down the cold-hearted riffles.

Custer's second-in-command, Major Joel Elliot, sees a half dozen young Cheyenne men leap onto ponies and tear off upstream. "Come on boys," he yells to his men. "Let's get 'em!" Twenty soldiers gallop in pursuit. "Here's to a promotion or a coffin," Elliot yells as they ride out of sight.

In the village, the fighting lasts only a few minutes. As final gunshots echo along the river, Custer gives orders to round up surviving women and children. His men are already dragging captured food, clothing, and blankets out of the tipis for burning.

They corral fifty-three captives, along with some eight hundred ponies that were grazing along the banks of the river. "We can't take those horses," Custer yells. Wiry "Indian" ponies tend to be too scrawny to make good cavalry horses.

Custer's adjutant, Lieutenant William Cooke, asks him, "What'll we do with them? We can't just let them go. The villages upstream will just take them."

Custer looks at him. "What villages?"

"There's a whole string of them. I rode upstream a little way and saw at least three more. They'll be down on us before long."

"Jesus," Custer says. "Where's Elliot?"

"Nobody's seen him since he took off after those riders."

Custer curses. The captive women and children huddle miserably, shivering in blankets before him. His men run in and out of tipis, stacking gear, getting it ready for burning. "All right," he commands. "Get enough blankets for these captives and pick out ponies for them to ride back to Camp Supply. Burn those tipis."

"What about the other horses?"

"We can't take them. You'll have to kill them." To punctuate his words, he draws his revolver and shoots a pony that's wandering among the tipis. Its back legs kick convulsively as the bullet strikes with an audible thump. It races fifty yards, then stumbles, falls, and lies with its hooves weakly flailing. "Tell the men to use sabers

or hatchets, whatever they have. Slit their throats if they can. Don't waste bullets."

Cooke trots away, gathers men; they set to the grisly task. Soon comes an eerie sound, ponies trumpeting their final breaths through slashed windpipes. The women hear it, too. They moan and tear their hair. Here and there, gunfire drifts through the air. Then there's the crackle of flame as the first tipis blaze up.

H Company commander, Captain Frederick Benteen, rides up. "Have you seen Elliot?" he asks. "He's still not back."

"Damn him," Custer says with a grimace. "He didn't ask me. He had no right." He spits out the next five words: "No. I haven't seen him."

"I'll take some men and see if I can find him."

"The hell you will. Your duty is here."

Benteen glares at Custer. "Look, Colonel, we need to find those men. We don't know, they could be in trouble."

"I'll worry about Elliot. You and your men have horses to kill."

Benteen's mouth works. He salutes and rides away, scowling. While the men destroy the village, Custer rides up a low hill that overlooks the river. He sees neither hide nor hair of Major Elliot or his men, but in the distance upstream he does see the tipis of another village. And another, tiny in the distance beyond that. He can see shapes, men on horses milling about.

Dammit, he thinks to himself. This is trouble. He gallops back. All about him, tipis, lodge poles, robes, hides, and blankets burn and crackle. The air stinks with burning meat and hair. "Cooke!" he screams.

Lieutenant Cooke canters up. "Form up the men," Custer shouts. "We've got to get out of here."

"What about Elliot?"

"That's too bad, but we don't want to be caught here. Or anywhere near here."

Cooke passes the orders along. Men organize and climb onto their horses. From the corner of his eye, Custer sees Benteen glaring at him. He ignores Benteen. In a half hour, the mighty 7th Cavalry starts back to Camp Supply, shielded from massing Cheyenne and Kiowa warriors by the women and children they hold hostage.

They arrive at Camp Supply the next day to find none other than General Philip Sheridan waiting for them. The timing is perfect. As military commander over the Western Territories, Sheridan had specifically requested Custer to lead this expedition. Custer is anxious to show he was the right choice. His success will lose nothing in the telling.

Two weeks later, Major Joel Elliot still has not turned up. A battalion of one hundred men ride back toward the Washita River to look for them. They find the bodies two miles from the burned village. The men had been surrounded and cut off, barely out of view from Custer and the rest of the battalion. Their frozen bodies had been stripped and mutilated. That's the way it is in the "Indian Wars." Quarter is rarely given on either side.

Joel Elliot was Captain Benteen's best friend. Benteen is distraught, but hardly surprised. How even Custer could ride away without even trying to find his own men—even Custer—how could a man do that?

Benteen stews. In an off hour, he pens a bitter letter to another friend, an officer stationed in St. Louis: How could even Custer spend half a day sampling the wares of the Cheyenne, admiring Cheyenne women, killing Cheyenne horses, yet never bother to search for his second-in-command and twenty fellow soldiers?

Unknown to Benteen, the friend passes the letter to a newspaper, which prints it.

Weeks after that, the bugler sounds Officers' Call in Custer's command tent. Benteen arrives late to find Custer pacing back and forth, yelling at his officers, whacking his riding boot with a quirt. "No officer is to write letters to newspapers," he shouts, even though he himself writes letters and magazine articles about his exploits all the time. "If I find out who did this, I'll cowhide that man within an inch of his life!"

Listening, Benteen understands that it was his letter that somehow made it into the press. He steps back out of the tent. Oil lanterns cast enough light outside for Benteen to draw his service revolver and make sure it's loaded. The cylinder clicks evilly as he turns it, like a neck being snapped. Holstering the weapon, he steps back in. "Colonel, I guess I'm the man you want. I'm ready for the whipping you promised."

Custer's mouth drops open. Benteen's eyes are pale blue, cold as a dagger chipping ice. The two men stare at each other. Custer's mouth works. Finally, he manages to say, "Benteen, I'll see you again." He throws the quirt onto his desk. "Dismissed."

Benteen glares at Custer as the other officers edge past him and out of the tent. Finally, he also turns on his heel and walks away.

Back East, newspapers love Custer's reports of his great victory on the Washita River. It makes his reputation as an "Indian fighter." But in a dozen years of warfare against the Nations of America's sprawling prairies, this is the only victory George Armstrong Custer ever wins.

THE CROW NATION

ile after mile, all the way from Ashfall Fossil Beds to the Black Hills, prairie horizons rolled in endless progression. The expanse isn't measureless from a weather satellite, of course, nor on a road map. But down on the ground, where I was driving, it certainly kept my mind on the big picture.

As a fourth-generation Euro-American, I was taught throughout my childhood that the *real* history of North America began in 1492. What came before was, it was at least implied, mere prelude. Subsequent learning, not to mention these rolling horizons, suggest that my educators got it precisely backwards. European occupation is postlude to a fifteen thousand-year (at least) ballet of indigenous cultural evolution.

Indigenous accounts, not to mention archaeological evidence, show that the original tenants were doing just fine before Columbus showed up. Seriously, now: horses, steel knives, rifles all come in handy. But do they replace freedom and self-realization? Could I think smallpox and cholera were gifts anybody wanted?

The list of diseases imported from Europe includes measles, scarlet fever, typhoid fever, typhus, influenza, pertussis, tuberculosis, and diphtheria. Expanding out of New England, colonists could tell themselves they were claiming vacant land precisely because their diseases had already wiped out many of their indigenous neighbors. Colonial documents also suggest they started some epidemics intentionally. It was an effective way to eliminate indigenous competition.

My school teachers also neglected to tell us, Manifest Destiny was really just a nice term for genocide. Each individual conquest might have seemed necessary enough at the time. But taken *en masse*—what enormity! It wasn't European intellectual or spiritual superiority that conquered the continent, but European epidemics and high-temperature metallurgy. It was done with chilling ease and no small amount of self-satisfied glibness. How easy, again, to practice ruthlessness and call it virtue.

In their 1823 decision, *Johnson v. M'Intosh*, which is still studied by first-year law students, the United States Supreme Court codified the perceived superiority of Euro-American culture and the Christian religion. The federal government had the right, the Court held, to occupy indigenous lands through conquest and the so-called Doctrine of Discovery. European civilization and Christianity brought such benefit, they held, as to compensate any loss of indigenous real estate. To this day, America's legal system has never rejected, repealed, or even questioned this doctrine of white supremacy. Once planted, the vines of bigotry do not uproot themselves.

Once they secured their conquest, Euro-Americans did build schools for First Nation children. But the schools had a strong missionary function. They outlawed indigenous religion and strictly enforced Christianity. It was also forbidden to speak any indigenous language, the speech of one's own parents.

Well into the twentieth century, beatings were common for children who disobeyed those rules. Considering that striking a child was almost unheard of among the Great Plains Nations, the effect of a beating on an "Indian school" student can only be imagined. Children regularly died from homesickness, rough treatment, and poor food.

As my great-grandparents' child, I have to marvel at the very survival of indigenous culture. Survivance. It sings the irrepressibility of the human spirit. Indigenous art and thought slip out from behind the glass of museum cases, name the ground we stand on, color the stones, and are increasingly recognized in general.

Native American scholar, Gerald Vizenor, suggests that this is the very spirit of survivance: for First Nations to reclaim their culture and history in their own terms, not the terms of the conquerors. How uncrushable is a human spirit that can do this, reclaiming old arts and traditions while struggling just to survive as strangers in this land made strange to them.

For all the bad things we do to each other, I also see the human experience as most wonderful in our capacity to overcome one another's crimes. Episodes such as Wounded Knee and the Washita are not comfortable heritage. But the human capacity to rebound from cultural—and physical—genocide provides a silver lining to the sorrow.

Pondering all this, just as a lens, I bought Frederick Hoxie's history of the Crow Nation, *Parading through History*. Plenty Coups's and Pretty Shield's people called themselves Absaalooke, which in their tongue means "Children of the Large-Beaked Bird." In what was to become routine European dismissal of indigenous cultural nuance, French fur trappers translated that as "Children of the Crow." The last word got handed down, so they have been known as the Crow ever since.

Anthropologists surmise that before Europeans arrived, the Crow lived in the Ohio River Valley. As European expansion pushed eastern Nations inland, the chain reaction pressed the Crow north and west. They slowly migrated all the way to what is now southern Canada, where they impinged on the Cheyenne. Both, in turn, were driven farther west by the "Sioux," an alliance of Nations speaking a common tongue.

I read that the word "Sioux" has been variously translated to mean "enemies," "little demons," or "little snakes." Today, some "Sioux" are okay with it. Others despise it. One alternative is their own word, *Oyate*, translated as "people" or "nation." There are three great divisions of the *Oyate* people, sometimes referred to as the Santee, the Yanktonai, and the Lakota.

As the Crow found themselves in bitter enmity with the *Oyate*, particularly the Lakota, they decided "Sioux" was just a dandy term. Unfortunately for the Crow, the *Oyate*, Cheyenne, and Arapahoe made peace with one another. All three turned on the Crow, forcing them even farther west and south, into what is now Wyoming and Montana.

There, the Crow ran up against the Blackfeet and Shoshone in a migratory chain reaction. At the Continental Divide, stymied by Nations to the west of them, the Crow were forced to stand fast, pinioned between contending cultures.

When the Spanish accidentally re-introduced horses into North America, the Crow were quick to adapt them. They became great horse breeders, horse riders, and most of all, horse warriors. Horses are still a big part of Crow culture. They were a strong Nation, they'll tell you, robustly defending themselves from all comers.

Then came that most potent European import, disease. The Crow turned out to be particularly susceptible. Smallpox hit in the early 1800s, and they never fully recovered. All the while, the Lakota and Cheyenne made constant war on them. By 1850 the Crow were definitely getting the worst of it.

BEARS

*B*ears were important to Crow life. When Plenty Coups faced the wounded buffalo, he steeled his courage by saying to himself, "I have the heart of a grizzly bear." His grandfather had actually killed a grizzly bear and given each village boy a raw piece of the heart to eat.

Likewise, Pretty Shield told Linderman stories about bears. In one, the village had just moved, the men had hurried off to hunt, and the women were rushing to set up camp. Nearby bushes hung heavy with ripe blackberries. Berry-picking needed to wait, though, while the women set up the lodges and pegged the buffalo-hide covers to the ground.

One woman, as Pretty Shield tells it, was in too great a hurry. She left her tipi unpegged and ran out with a basket to get the sweetest berries. Pretty Shield and her mother were hurrying to finish when they heard the woman's screams. She was being attacked by a bear.

Pretty Shield's mother rushed Pretty Shield and her sister into their tipi and hid them beneath a buffalo robe. The children could hear the woman's screams. Pretty Shield told

Linderman poignantly how her sister began to cry with fright, and how Pretty Shield tried to calm her by singing to her. But Pretty Shield said she herself was so terrified, she couldn't make a sound.

One warrior, left to guard the village, rushed the bear from behind and stabbed it with his knife, so that the woman was able to escape. He held it off long enough until some hunters returned and helped him kill it.

The mauled woman made it as far as Pretty Shield's tipi, where she collapsed and died in front of them. Years later, talking to Linderman, Pretty Shield made sense of this tragedy by supposing the bear had been the woman's punishment. She had rushed to hoard berries meant for the whole village, Pretty Shield said. Horrible as the death was, it gained meaning this way. Bears were a part of nature. To Pretty Shield, the broad spectrum of nature taught the people how to live. Through her story ran the thread of commonality with one's neighbor, and also with the surrounding world in which survival depended on cooperation.

Pretty Shield witnessed the most violent forms of death, yet she never showed signs of lingering trauma. Neither did Plenty Coups. They insisted, in fact, that the Crow were free of infirmity before whites forced them to become "civilized." To hear it from their point of view, indigenous children survived wild animals, runaway horses, and inter-tribal warfare with relative aplomb. It was white mission schools that did them in.

Pretty Shield told another bear story. She was fourteen, a young woman ready to marry. She and her friends were far from camp, digging turnips. She was wearing a new buckskin dress, which she and her mother had labored over for weeks.

She glanced up to see four men riding horses slowly

down a nearby mountainside. Thinking they were Lakota, she yelled a warning. She and her friends shinnied up nearby ponderosa pines and hid in the branches.

They quickly recognized the riders as young men from their own village, laughing uproariously because they had roped a mother bear and two cubs. The youths were dragging the beasts behind their horses, working the horses, pulling the mother bear off her feet each time she tried to attack.

One thing led to another, the young women and young men yelling and teasing one another. When the young women refused to climb down, the lads tied the bears to the trees in which the females sat. Then they rode away, laughing at the shouts and screams behind them.

It was a hot day, not a breath of air, and it was miserable clinging to rough tree branches. The pines were sticky with sap. The bears growled and snapped at their ropes and a sickening bear smell wafted up to Pretty Shield. Worst of all, the pine sap got all over her new buckskin dress and ruined it.

After a long time, Pretty Shield's father once more showed up. He apparently got wind of the prank and made the boys return and free the bears. Even as the bears ran away, the boys were still giggling. When Pretty Shield's father added his own laughter, her misery and anger overcame her. Furious from the prank and the wreckage of her ruined dress, she burst into tears.

According to Linderman she screamed at the boys, "You could be dying with your belly cut open. Then I could laugh at you." Which, one suspects, only made them laugh the harder. It did, however, put a stop to her father's amusement.

Years later, talking to Linderman, she could finally see the humor. Then she said something which, to me, is crucial: "Now I laugh sometimes. Bad things happen. You can't make

119

them un-happen. What can you do but look back years later and smile?"

Survivance. I wonder how much her statement embodies First Nations' swim across Manifest Destiny's deluge. Watching Euro-American culture suck uranium from beneath the land where their forebears hunted buffalo, watching oil pipes cross it, nuclear missile silos dug into it, oil refineries, concrete, asphalt, and stockyards all over it, First Nations would have an excuse to die from anger. But they have endured, often with wry laughter. Like the Navajo movie extras, enjoying ribald humor at Hollywood director John Ford's ignorance of their language.

A GREAT DREAM

By the time Plenty Coups was ten years old, the Crow people had been resisting the Lakota, Cheyenne, and Arapahoe for a generation. The Cheyenne were fiercest, but the Lakota were most numerous. The Lakota had bartered many rifles from white traders, the Crow had only a few. Plenty Coups considered the bow and arrow superior for hunting, but rifles were an advantage in war. The Crow were ever more hard-pressed. They could never sleep soundly at night, Plenty Coups told Linderman, for fear of a Lakota raid.

He told Linderman of his tenth summer, camped beside the Yellowstone River. A crier rode through the village one morning, calling the young men to go out and dream.

Plenty Coups was already a leader among the village boys. The fate of his people heavy upon him, he and four friends bathed with sweet herbs, and set out without food or water. They walked for two days, to a peak called Crazy Mountain.

They fasted and wandered almost a week. Great leaders

must sacrifice for great dreams, so Plenty Coups left his friends behind, took out his knife, and cut off the end of his left index finger. Blood spattered a trail along the ground, then he collapsed.

He woke to see four eagles sitting in a tree, silently watching his blood trail. He and the eagles just stared at one another for a long time. The sun crawled across the sky. At last his friends came along and carried him back to camp.

About midnight a voice called him, and he saw a magical Person waiting for him, far away. It would have been several days' travel in waking life, but his dream crossed the distance in an instant. The Person showed him a vast plain teeming with buffalo. Then he was among the beasts, smelling them, feeling their rough bodies against him. The Person took out a rattle, shook it, and a hole opened in the ground. The buffalo disappeared down the hole one by one, faster and faster, till they had all vanished. A new kind of creature climbed out of the hole. Ten-year-old Plenty Coups had no idea what this new animal was called, nor what it meant.

Then the Person showed Plenty Coups a tall forest, blown down by Bad Storms till only one tree remained. In that tree's branches nested a small bird, the black-capped chickadee. Next, the Person showed him a tipi from which issued the sound of a baby laughing, and told him never to enter it. Finally, the Person showed him an old man sitting in the grass beside a small pond. Plenty Coups felt compassion for the man, he was so old and feeble. To Plenty Coups's surprise, the Person informed him that he, Plenty Coups, was that old man. Then the Person vanished.

Plenty Coups understood what chickadee meant in his vision. The Crow consider the chickadee the wisest of all creatures. Tiny though it is, it listens and learns from the mistakes of others. If the chickadee was to be his medicine animal, he jokingly said to Linderman, at least he would only have to carry a small medicine bundle.

But the rest of the dream was a mystery to him.

WISE ONES

*P*lenty Coups told Lindermen how his friends killed a deer and brought him meat and water. Again, reading his account, these were ten-year-old kids! Questing, days' travel from their parents, cutting off fingers, killing deer. A century and a half later, I'm still in awe of these children. Nowadays a parent can practically get arrested for letting a ten-year-old child take the subway alone.

Tradition seems to have dictated what followed. Plenty Coups' friends fetched tribal elders and they bore him back to the village, singing and celebrating. He was not allowed to talk to anyone till he had taken another purifying sweat bath. Then his uncles escorted him to an assembly of the village's Wise Ones.

Reading Plenty Coups's account of the Wise Ones' lodge, it is full of spirit and a kind of intimacy. It strikes me that in telling Linderman of it, he signified trust and appreciation for the respect Linderman had shown him. Plenty Coups even mentioned it broke a taboo to speak the names of people who had died. Plenty Coups was holding nothing back. To me, this came of his desire for white people to understand the Crow, to appreciate their deep reality as a people.

Sitting in a circle, the Wise Ones silently passed the medicine pipe. Plenty Coups waited and watched. Finally, the leader asked him to tell his dream, which he did. Then the pipe went around again. After long silence, just men drawing on the pipe, the leader proclaimed it "a great dream."

The war eagles gave Plenty Coups nothing, the leader explained. Fighting would not save the Crow people. The buffalo in the dream meant that the buffalo would go away forever during Plenty Coups' lifetime. They would be replaced by the white people's cattle, which were still new to the plains. A few of the elders had seen them, though Plenty Coups had not.

The Crow faced a grim prospect, the leader pronounced. Their way of life was dying in front of them; there was no hope in the old ways. The white people were the storm, destroying all First Nations mistaken enough to oppose them. The Crow were a small people, like the chickadee bird, so their hope lay in the chickadee's strength. They had to learn from the mistakes of their enemies, join forces with the whites, and keep peace with them at all costs.

The rest was personal to Plenty Coups. He would live to be an old man, have many victories, and someday live in a "square house," like the white people. He would never have children of his own. The Crow people's needs would be his children.

The leader finished speaking and the elder's voices filled the tipi, discussing the dream. Finally they passed the pipe to Plenty Coups, and the boy drew on it for the first time.

KNOWLEDGE IS SORROW

"$\mathcal{K}$nowledge is sorrow," writes Lakota political cartoonist, Marty Two Bulls, Sr. That's how he sums up a graphic feature in *Indian Country Today* magazine, in which he recounts the Lakota Black Snake Prophesy.

The Black Snake Prophesy provided the appellation used by First Nations and, later, environmental opponents to the Dakota Access Pipeline. As Two Bulls tells it, in the early twentieth century, a Lakota elder prophesied that a "… black snake … will cross our lands, killing all it touches, and in its passing the water will become poison."

The prophesy may really have happened, though more skeptical indigenous voices dismiss it as, at best, a story redacted for effect. Applying a new episode to an old text is a spiritual tradition across many cultures. Biblical scholars also cite passages where a story from one age was inserted into a much older scripture.

Whatever the origins of the Black Snake Prophesy, Marty Two Bulls's article got my attention. "Knowledge is sorrow," he wrote. I came of age in the scientifically heady 1950s and

'60s. My childhood didn't dream there was a downside to fossil fuel development, the uranium atom, artificial hydrocarbons, or consumer economic development. I grew up in happy faith that "knowledge is power."

Speaking of the Bible, *Genesis* does hint at the sorrowful, loss of innocence that comes with broadened knowledge. I find symbolized in Eve and Adam's expulsion from Eden the knowledge a child gains when it realizes adults can disappoint it, even hurt it. Later, world-weary *Ecclesiastes* puts it in so many words: "He who increases knowledge, increases sorrow."

Minority voice though it may be, then, knowledge as sorrow has a deep cross-cultural history. It only seemed new to me,

Two Bulls adds something. "Knowledge is sorrow, but hope lies with the wisdom to live and love." There is, to me, a kind of Zen to that statement. I've heard Dharma Masters refer to, "great love, great sadness, great Bodhisattva way."

For me, this could characterize Pretty Shield's final acceptance of the bears, or even what she had to say about Euro-Americans killing off the buffalo. I see it in the Crow Wise Ones' understanding that their way of life was dying, and that tribal policy must adapt to their limited means. In short, it strikes me that their *knowledge* of their own state and what it demands of them *is the existential sorrow of the disempowered*. Not just indigenous peoples, but ethnically and economically disadvantaged people in many contexts.

Reflecting, I see something important here. The foundational wisdom of survivance is the inner strength to "live and love" in the face of that which cannot be overcome by direct means. The day may arrive when Euro-American dominant culture finds itself in those same seas. That makes this a time to learn from those people whom Manifest Destiny's spirit glibly dismissed as not worth listening to.

PSYCHOLOGICAL MAGIC

*C*hief Plenty Coups was born in 1848. He grew up to fight battles, count coup on opposing warriors, and make no mistake, take many scalps. I don't pretend deep understanding of the world he grew up in. Nor would I have long survived in it.

But First Nations were expected to adapt, learn, and easily understand the industrialized, Euro-American world. Again and again, trying to rear her grandchildren in the 1920s, Pretty Shield would tell Linderman, "I do not understand these times. I am walking in the dark."

My Euro-American descent shapes me, but I have never felt particular guilt at the Native American genocide. Nor have I ever read or talked to a person of indigenous descent who desired me to feel guilt. I do feel a kind of sorrow, also an abiding sense of humility at my own cultural cluelessness, at what's easy to assume without even realizing I'm assuming. At memory lapses, unspoken re-acceptance of *privilege* relative to the disempowered as *a just and natural way of things*. (Like, say, the cultural imperialism at the core of American property law.)

I feel sorrow, compassion, respect, not just for what indigenous peoples lost—though that is truly poignant—but mostly for what they managed to retain and rebuild. Repeatedly, I find that groups with a history of oppression are greater than what was done to them. Which is precisely why they have something to teach dominant culture.

Perusing online for context about Plenty Coups and his dreams, what should I stumble onto but a segment of an Australian radio program, *The Philosopher Zone,* featuring an interview with University of Chicago philosophy professor, Jonathan Lear. The conversation was mainly about what Plenty Coups *wouldn't* talk about. The old chief refused to comment on his reservation life after "the buffalo went away." "After that, nothing happened," Plenty Coups told Linderman. "You can tell about that part of my life as well as I can."

Lear takes that as the embodiment of what he calls, "cultural devastation"; that is, a way of life so shattered, there are no longer even reference points to describe it. The interview moved me to order a copy of Lear's book, *Radical Hope: Ethics in the Face of Cultural Devastation.*

Crow community was close-knit, their anxiety deep and collective. To Lear, Plenty Coups' medicine dreams were a crucial tool by which they could adapt to the coming demise of their way of life. The dreams weren't magical in the "abracadabra" sense, but they were "strong medicine" in a psychological sense.

That set my brain clicking. Lear, a respected Western philosopher, draws wisdom from indigenous oral history. Acknowledging that much depends on the accuracy of Linderman's ear and shorthand, we can still watch Plenty Coups's story become myth in the large sense, a journey from lived experience into understanding deeper than the experience itself. The Crow guided themselves, using a kind of intuitive, communal wisdom which Euro-American technological individualism seems to lack.

As a fan of the sciences, I've read studies of dream research and the nature of memory. There are reams of data on memory's slippery, evolving nature, even as I acknowledge the imprecision of applying Western calipers to First Nations' oral tradition. But I believe some ways of knowing transcend culture. They provide a broad commonality from which twenty-first century technocrats might learn a thing or two.

Abundant research suggests to me how, each time Plenty Coups described his dream, he drew from long-term memory, ran the story through short-term memory to talk about it, then put it back, altered in the process. Cut-and-dried though memory seems, it's an evolving thing. Discussion and experience bend it in new directions.

I therefore question whether the dream Plenty Coups really experienced was the dream he remembered after the Wise Ones re-described it for him. I suggest that it had likely evolved even more by the time he recounted it to Linderman seventy years later.

By the time Plenty Coups described his dream to Linderman, he had been recalling and discussing it for a lifetime. Crow life was collective, their concern about their future was collective. I believe Plenty Coup's medicine dream was also collective. It was a process that drew wisdom from the whole tribal council, including discussions that were going on before Plenty Coups even went to Crazy Mountain.

As one example of how I believe this worked, ten-year-old Plenty Coups had never seen white people's cattle. But the Wise Ones' leader had. He interpreted the unknown creatures in Plenty Coups's dream in his own terms, feeding that image back into the boy's memory as Euro-American cattle.

The Crow were hard-pressed by the Cheyenne and Lakota even before Euro-American settlers and the US Army came into the picture. Crow elders had no illusions about resisting Euro-American steel, steam, and gunpowder. Particularly given their struggles against the Cheyenne and Lakota, the Crow's best option for cultural survival lay in alliance with the whites, however difficult that might be. Plenty Coups' medicine dream evolved into a perfect vehicle to express that strategy. I believe the dream's collective imagery and language embodied a policy that was already decided.

Jonathan Lear's book doesn't mention the volatile dynamics of memory, but he does discuss the role Plenty Coups's dreams played in the Crow's adjustment to the changes they saw coming. It was communal use of what Lear calls, "existing folkways."

As Lear puts it, the Crow knew their hunter-gatherer-warrior lifestyle was not sustainable. They therefore took advantage of a "folkway," their medicine dream tradition, to form a workable policy. Psychological symbolism became real-world strategy in a way that was arguably ahead of Euro-American culture's long-term planning, even today. These were smart, sophisticated people, practicing survivance one hundred fifty years before that term was even coined.

Beginning in the mid-1990s, indigenous scholar and activist, Gerald Vizenor, was the first to apply the term survivance to the indigenous experience. Writing a decade later, Lear gives no sign he has ever heard the term. Yet analyzing the Crow's tribal strategy through the lens of Western philosophy, he describes the same thing.

It seems to me that when two cultures arrive in the same place from manifestly different approaches, it's worth paying attention.

ROSEBUD

*B*oth Plenty Coups and Pretty Shield told stories about what's sometimes called the Black Hills War of the 1870s. Euro-Americans wanted the Black Hills. The Lakota and Cheyenne vowed to expel the invaders or go down fighting. To save as much of their own land and culture as possible, the Crow allied with the whites.

Pretty Shield told how her village sent many men to help the US Army's General George Crook, whom they called, "Three Stars." They also sent six men to scout for General Alfred Terry, who was leading another column of troops down from the northeast. Terry wound up passing all six Crow scouts along to George Custer's 7th Cavalry. One of the scouts, Goes Ahead, was Pretty Shield's husband.

She mentions Plenty Coups as a leader renowned for skill and bravery by that time. He led one hundred thirty Crow warriors with Three Stars Crook. A force of Shoshone allies also joined them. Plenty Coups fondly remembered to Linderman the military pageantry as Crow and Shoshone warriors joined the white soldiers at Fort Fetterman. It was a day of parades.

But Pretty Shield surprised me with an angle the men didn't talk about, which I never suspected. Among the Crow who fought alongside Three Stars were two women. One, The-Other-Magpie, she described as a woman of great beauty whose brother had been killed by the Lakota. The other was, as Pretty Shield termed it, a "half-woman," called Finds-Them-and-Kills-Them. As Pretty Shield put it, Finds-Them-and-Kills-Them had the body of a man, but the clothing and heart of a woman. Given current twenty-first century struggles to accommodate, or even describe, non-binary gender identities, I once more marvel at the cultural sophistication in Pretty Shield's matter-of-fact narrative.

Three Stars Crook marched north to Rosebud Creek in Montana, with twelve hundred soldiers. They were eating breakfast beside their tents when Crazy Horse attacked at the head of a thousand Lakota warriors.

Unlike the white soldiers, the Crow and Shoshone were alert and prepared. While the surprised bluecoats scrambled for weapons, the Crow and Shoshone held off Crazy Horse's men. In the end, Crazy Horse won and Three Stars Crook had to retreat south for reinforcements. But it would have been much worse, had not the Crow and Shoshone filled the breach while the white soldiers ran to pick up their rifles.

Plenty Coups gives an exciting account of the fighting. It was a glorious time for the Crows, despite the bluecoats' losses and retreat. The Crow fought hard, took scalps, and returned to their people for a victory dance.

But Pretty Shield's descriptions of The-Other-Magpie's and Finds-Them-and-Kills-Them's exploits are the more fascinating. Both women fought magnificently.

Carrying only a coup stick, The-Other-Magpie counted coup on multiple Lakota men. My Western lack of under-standing for Crow ethics glares through the fact that it took me a year to comprehend what Pretty Shield was driving at.

To my Euro-American mind, it made no sense that she carried no weapon, only a coup stick.

A coup stick is a wooden pole, perhaps four or five feet long, sometimes decorated with beads or feathers. It is not a weapon. Rather, touching an enemy with it in battle without killing him is an act of paramount courage. The coup stick itself is kept as a record of such achievements, in the form of notches or eagle feathers fastened along its length.

Only slowly did I realize Pretty Shield was holding The-Other-Magpie up as the bravest person on the field that day —as a woman. She gained her revenge purely through honor, counting coup. As a woman, weapons of war weren't her business. But in counting coup without carrying a weapon, she was courageous without match.

Meanwhile, Finds-Them-and-Kills-Them expected to be killed. "It is a good day to die." In her man's body, Pretty Shield told Linderman, she feared the Lakota might take woman's clothing as cause to mutilate her body, to keep her spirit from going to the next world. She wore men's clothes, carried a rifle, and used it to deadly effect.

When a Crow named Bull Snake fell, badly wounded, Finds-Them-And-Kills-Them jumped from her horse and stood over him, firing at the enemy. The-Other-Magpie joined her, lashing about with her coup stick, defying the hail of Lakota bullets. Pretty Shield exalted to Linderman how strong was their fighting medicine that day. They saved Bull Snake to return to his people.

I can only try to imagine how a transgender person would have fared with General Crook or Colonel Custer. Had Finds-Them-And-Kills-Them been white, life with Crook's army would have been lonely, even deadly. Given the precarious lot of transgender people in Euro-American culture even now, Pretty Shield's story is one more example of how much First Nations have to teach.

The-Other-Magpie did take one scalp, which Pretty Shield said she later saw. During the celebration dance, The-Other-Magpie cut the scalp into pieces, so more Crow men would have a scalp to dance with.

I picture Pretty Shield's eyes flashing as she told Linderman how two women fought at the Battle of the Rosebud. She finished by adding, "The men never talk about this."

STRONG AND SACRED MEDICINE

*E*ven by freeway, traveling half the state of Wyoming is a long way. Across the miles, I ruminated on that skull young Pretty Shield dug up and showed her father. I'm not sure twenty-first-century scientific replicability has anything to do with their way of understanding what the girls had found. I would bet that if you showed the skull to paleontologist Mike Voorhies, he could quickly proclaim it a mammoth or giant ground sloth or short-faced bear. All of them were around as recently as the Hudson-Meng site, shallow fossils that kids with root-diggers could stumble upon.

I acknowledge that explanation. But at their best, I see science and myth dwelling in creative tension. The skull's scientific reality does not negate it as a living poem of life, death, and hugeness. I find it wonderful that Pretty Shield's father brought out his medicine pipe, sent the kids away, and sat smoking with it. I love the way he wrapped it in a good buffalo robe and reverently re-buried it. I totally "get" that. I bet Mike Voorhies would, too.

Pretty Shield's father didn't know paleontology, but he

knew reverence, the living mystery embodied by that skull. The reverent act isn't just about the item, after all. It's also about the act's effect on the reverent person: not important because of any magical result, but an act of "worship" that changes the worshipper in important ways.

We are part of worlds that came and went long before we got here. We're part of a world which will endure, ever changing, long after we're gone. I read about Pretty Shield's father, or even look at Mike Voorhies' Columbian mammoth, and feel the hugeness that lies beyond self. I am not a smoker. But drawing a card from the Crow Wise Ones' deck, I would have been honored to light up out of respect. Pretty Shield's father knew a temple is where you find it. He carried his incense with him.

In 1930, almost to the end of Linderman's book of interviews with him, Plenty Coups sat on the long front porch of his "square house" near Montana's Pryor Creek. After his account of the Battle of the Rosebud, he told Linderman about the battle at the Greasy Grass River, which took place a week later. Greasy Grass is the Great Plains Nations' name for the Little Bighorn, where the Cheyenne and Lakota killed Custer. Plenty Coups used the Crow name for Custer, Son-of-the-Morning-Star.

Son-of-the-Morning-Star was foolish, Plenty Coups said. He insulted his Crow scouts and was too arrogant to heed their warnings. If he had listened and kept his force together, Plenty Coups opined, Custer and his men might have lived.

Still, Plenty Coups considered Son-of-the-Morning-Star a brave man who died a brave death. It made all the Crow sad to hear of it. But "that fighting and our fighting with Three Stars Crook broke the backs of the Cheyenne and Lakota," Plenty Coups said, "I am proud to have been part of that." With the demise of their enemies, the Crow could at last sleep unafraid.

"Sleeping unafraid" came at a price, though. Plenty Coups spoke poignantly of the changes that came to the Crow, too, after the Great Plains War. The buffalo were soon all killed, as the Crow leaders had foretold in Plenty Coups' dream. Hunting, war parties, and horse stealing fell out of Crow life. White people spread everywhere. Even though the Crow were resolved to be friendly with the whites, Plenty Coups said, it was difficult. "White people often speak one thing and do another," he said, "promise one thing and then forget they made a promise."

He recited a litany of white perversity. Whites expected the Crow to obey white laws, while breaking them themselves. Whites told the Crow not to drink whiskey, he said, then traded whiskey to them for furs till the fur animals were nearly wiped out. White missionaries preached to the Crow, but white people themselves couldn't agree which religion was right. The Crow saw how whites didn't obey their own religion any more than their own laws.

Plenty Coups told Linderman that the Crow kept their word even when it was hard. "The white man . . . is like a god in some ways but foolish —foolish—in others. He fools nobody but himself."

So there. As a Euro-American, I blush inside. Plenty Coups knew who he was and also those with whom he dealt, even as his world shifted on its axis. A hundred years later, his words still ring true. Reflecting on this, I will go outside my own "square house" to walk in the woods. I will ponder the great forces and wonders about me, and living things, and death. I will love and grieve the triumphs and tragedies of my fellow human beings. Life is teaching me that I, too, am capable of fooling nobody but myself.

Then again, reading some things Pretty Shield had to say about Plenty Coups, he fooled himself from time to time, as well. That makes me feel better.

PART IV
PARANOIA

May we engage life so as to see not just the wonder, but also the horror. For . . . it is in the face of the world's heartbreaks that the heart beats most courageously.

—Thoughts from a Gentle Atheist

IN THE MATTER OF THE LITTLE BIGHORN

*H*alfway across Wyoming, Interstate 90 veers north into southern Montana. My next stop was Little Bighorn Battlefield National Monument, where Custer met his demise. I resolved to spend no more than a morning there. It didn't seem right to spend more time with Custer than I had at Wounded Knee.

Scion of the Rocky Mountain West that I am, I've been reading about Custer ever since elementary school. One fascinating source is the transcript of the army's Court of Inquiry, now available online. It reads almost like a play, and has, in fact, been turned into drama.

Setting: Chicago. Year: 1879. Month: January. *The day is as cold and hard as the ice on Lake Michigan. The grand ballroom of Chicago's Palmer House hotel teems with military men in mature deliberation.*

They've roped back the velvet curtains to let in natural light. That doesn't help much, it's a shadowy day, snowflakes drift past the windows. Cast iron radiators throb along the wainscoting, but the people in the room keep bundled up anyway. Ornate designs twine up the wallpaper toward a ceiling mural laced with genuine gold florets. Gaslights flicker down the center of the room.

The whole Palmer house exudes Victorian opulence and propriety, which is exactly the tone the US Army wants. This Court of Inquiry comes not of Army concern about the debacle at the Little Bighorn, but of civilian controversy.

Despite his gift for publicity, Custer's military skills were mediocre at best. Custer's army superiors knew him for what he was: courageous and aggressive, yes, but egotistical, unpredictable, and sometimes downright erratic. President Ulysses S. Grant summed Custer's death up for a newspaper reporter. "I regard Custer's Massacre was a sacrifice of troops, brought on by Custer himself, that was wholly unnecessary—wholly unnecessary." The government felt no need for an inquiry.

That ran afoul of public opinion, though. Primed on Custer's writings the way Donald Trump fans were primed on *The Apprentice,* the masses saw Custer as the invincible "Indian fighter." They were stunned by his demise.

What's more, neither Grant nor the army planned on Custer's wife, Elizabeth. Being the Colonel's wife was "Libbie" Custer's life calling, and she was not about to let that work be dismissed. With iron will and canny strategy, she set about turning her husband's flawed life into legend. She tirelessly wrote books and gave lectures, playing on public opinion. Their marriage became the stuff of romance and drama, with Custer portrayed as the gallant martyr, betrayed by slacker officers.

One fervent follower was a dime novelist named Frederick Whittaker. He borrowed Libbie Custer's notes and letters to produce a hot-selling potboiler, the first Custer biography. Like her, Whittaker declared Custer's demise the sole product of his officers' cowardice and betrayal.

Their chief scapegoat was Major Marcus Reno. Not satisfied with the charges in his fanciful book, Whittaker wrote Congress to accuse Reno of cowardice, drunkenness, and dereliction of duty. Newspapers got ahold of the charges. It was then that Reno, dark of complexion and fortune alike, asked for the Court of Inquiry to save what little remained of his reputation.

Major Reno, ill at ease, sits with his lawyer at a long table. Reno takes careful notes as each witness testifies, almost all of them 7th Cavalry troopers. They don't look any happier to be there than Reno is. At the front of the room, the three-general court doesn't look like they want to be there, either. The audience, though, is standing-room-only. A squad of newspaper reporters scribble down every word.

Testimony tells how, for days, the 7th Cavalry followed the churned tracks and drag marks of an immense "Sioux" and Cheyenne migration. The trail was a mile wide in some places, carved three feet into the prairie soil. Hot on this trail, Custer drove his men all night to catch up. During a pause the morning of June 26th, their six Crow scouts climbed a nearby hill and informed Custer they could see the enemy camp in the distance. It was, they said, the largest camp they had ever seen. Joining them atop the hill, Custer looked through his spyglass, snickered, and told the scouts they were mistaken. He saw nothing but dust rising off the valley floor.

The Crow scouts, being "Indians," were not invited to testify at the Court of Inquiry. No one heard their opinions of Custer or his tactics, or how insulted they felt when he pooh-poohed them. Nor did the court hear how the scouts' leader, Half-Yellow-Face, informed Custer in sign language that if he attacked that camp, "You and I will go home tonight by a road we do not know." No one mentioned, but the scouts always insisted, Custer was sipping liquor out of "a little yellow bottle" all morning. "Indian" opinions were not considered relevant to the army's deliberations.

OF MEN AND MYTHS

*J*read somewhere that more has been written about George Armstrong Custer than any other American in history with the sole exception of Abraham Lincoln. I haven't personally verified this. I do know I could have gone broke buying all the Custer books I've come across. Likewise, I've web-surfed unlimited blogs, transcripts, and videos about Custer's Last Stand.

A lot of what gets written about Custer is pure horse-feathers. As one instance, the raid on the Washita River was one of very few instances where the Great Plains Nations *didn't* make a fool of Custer. Fighting Cheyenne, Kiowa, and Lakota was nothing like his Civil War years, where pure aggressiveness on battlefields laid out by more able minds, had given him a dashing reputation.

The transcript of Reno's Court of Inquiry also impressed me as much by what the witnesses *didn't* talk about as what they did. For example, there was little mention that the week before, Crazy Horse and his warriors had mauled and sent packing a force twice as powerful as Custer's.

Some soldiers remarked on Reno's drinking and conduct

outside the courtroom, but in front of reporters and the officers of the court, they kept mum. Army commissary records show that whiskey consumption was high throughout the 7th Cavalry. It was a culture of hard drinkers, Reno particularly so. But only two civilian contract employees, "packers" who took care of the mule train, were willing to accuse Reno on the record. Same thing with the issue of cowardice. Under oath, none of Reno's fellow soldiers were willing to fault him. To go by their testimony about one another, the soldiers were all sober and each one did his duty courageously.

Drawing from archives and archeological evidence, I learned that a third of the 7th Cavalry were raw recruits. Some had never even fired a military rifle and could barely ride an army horse. That tidbit didn't come up at the Court of Inquiry, either.

But the largest invisible specter, lurking behind every exchange, was hatred between the senior officers. The Washita River raid and Custer's desertion of Major Joel Elliot lay like pestilence over Custer, Reno, and Captain Benteen.

Son of the Morning Star, Evan S. Connell's massive compendium of all things Custer, describes Benteen's look as "the iron-gray eyes of a killer." I don't know what Connell means. Using crime writer Jay Robert Nash's three-volume collection of criminal biographies, *Bloodletters and Bad Men*, I examined many photographs of killers to see if I could understand. I found all kinds of different eyes.

Witnesses did, however, attest to Benteen's steely courage. The record shows he would kill when duty called for it. What I mainly see in old photographs of Benteen is a man who did not suffer fools easily, and who did not long ponder before assigning someone to that category. He detested Custer. He made no bones about it in letters or his testimony. He seems to have barely tolerated Reno.

Custer did have admirers, his relatives chief among them. Some followed Custer into military life and became officers in his regiment. His adjutant, Lieutenant Cooke, also adored him. His youngest brother and also his nephew had never joined the army. But against regulations, even though neither had ever even been to Montana, Custer got them both hired as "scouts" for the 1876 expedition. Custer's favoritism was shameless, but his inner circle worshiped him. To those outside that charmed circle, Custer spoke barely a word. The "Custer Clan," as non-members called them, rode together, partied together, and died together.

By the morning of June 26th, testimony runs, the 7th Cavalry had been passing huge, abandoned campsites for days. They spotted stray warriors in the distance. As they closed in, Custer detached Benteen with one hundred twenty-five men, to search a line of bluffs far to the south. This even though there was no sign of any trail other than the one they were following. Benteen saw no use to it and protested, but Custer's orders were set in stone.

Miles later, descending into the Little Bighorn Valley, Custer detached Major Reno with another one hundred ten men to attack the east end of the camp. Meanwhile, the pack train had fallen far behind. Custer's force was, therefore, catastrophically divided. With fewer than seven hundred men to begin with, they were now in four separate groups, none of whom even knew where the others were. Finally, with his favored circle and about two hundred men, Custer circled northwest. At no point did he hint to anyone outside the Custer Clan what his plans were. If he even had plans.

That was another thread I found. Custer was a martinet who never explained his intentions to his senior officers. He expected them to obey without question. The only reason I can see for Custer to send Benteen off south was to keep Custer's most despised enemy from the glory Custer expected to gain when he cornered the "Indians."

Ordered to attack, Reno thought Custer would back him up.

But Custer disappeared over the ridge and out of sight. Then a thousand warriors boiled out of the camp and overwhelmed Reno's puny charge, driving them back in disarray. With no idea where Custer was or what Custer intended, Reno cut his losses and retreated pell-mell to a hilltop a mile away. Both Benteen's battalion and the pack train stumbled across them later in the day. That's where those three units spent the next day and a half, cowering beneath a hail of Native bullets and arrows.

The Inquiry grinds on for weeks, as newspapers breathlessly print every word. Whittaker's sunken, mustached face grows more furious with each failure by the court to pillory Reno more satisfactorily. Whittaker sends the court a list of questions to put to Reno, and demands to do the cross-examination himself. The court accepts the questions, but they politely decline his offer to lead the prosecution. Outraged, Whittaker condemns the inquiry as a "methodical whitewash," and takes a train home. Twenty years later, he will gun himself down, either by accident or on purpose, in the stairwell of his New York house.

Captain Benteen takes the witness stand. He cuts an impressive figure, Benteen, and his testimony is full of acid one-liners. He refers to Custer's orders sending him south as "valley hunting ad infinitum," and dismisses it as "rather a senseless order." Coming upon Reno's men, besieged on their desolate hilltop, he offers with dry understatement, "They all thought there was a happier place than that, I guess." Later, as to Reno's drinking, "If I had known he had any [whiskey] on him, I'd have been after some myself." He gives Reno his due, though with faint praise. Asked of Reno's performance under fire, he replies, "I think it was all right."

Most telling is Benteen's reply when the court's officer asks him where he thought Custer might be during the siege. I picture his glare. "It was the belief of the officers on the hill that General Custer had gone [on to the Yellowstone River] and we were abandoned to our fate." In other words, the besieged men believed that Custer left them to die. Same as he had left Major Elliot and his men to die at the Washita.

Benteen completed his testimony by describing the scene two days later, when he finally saw the bodies on Custer's end of the battlefield. Custer and his men lay in no order, Benteen said. "I have seen rows of thrown corn, scattered that exact same way."

I tried to conjure Benteen's expression, telling how his men had to bury bodies that had lain in the summer sun for two days. For all his contempt for Custer, Benteen's emotions are hard to picture. He believed Custer had abandoned him and Reno to be slaughtered. Instead, it was Custer and his men who were slaughtered. Could Benteen have been unmoved?

Reno asks to take the stand. His account is much like Benteen's. Directly asked about his relationship with Custer, Reno is wary. He has already run afoul of Custer's fanatical supporters, so he dodges the question. The army's attorney repeats himself, and again Reno sidesteps. Finally the court insists and Reno replies, "Well, sir; I had known General Custer a long time, and I had no confidence in his ability as a soldier. I had known him all through the war."

On the trail, then, of perhaps ten thousand "Sioux" and Cheyenne, two thousand of them seasoned warriors armed to the teeth, Custer split his men into four small groups, none of whom knew where the others were. Custer told no one what his strategy was, if he even had one. The relationship between Custer and his senior officers was steeped in dysfunction: assumptions of worst intentions on everyone's part. I reflect that Custer and his men died as much from paranoia as from Lakota and Cheyenne arrows and bullets.

I feel the most sympathy for Reno. Abundant witnesses have described how the onslaught from the camp drove him and his men back. Surrounded, he had turned to question an Arikara scout named Bloody Knife, just as a bullet struck

Bloody Knife in the back of the head. Blood and brains exploded across Reno's face.

Evan Connell proposes that Reno may have suffered from post-traumatic stress disorder as far back as the Civil War, when he had led a company of Union Army soldiers into a Confederate Army trap. If that didn't do the trick, the episode with Bloody Knife certainly did. Reno became erratic and indecisive. Not that he was the only one. In conversations and letters, survivors describe several of Reno's men, besieged on their remote hilltop, "blubbering like babies."

Yet to judge by the men's testimony, every soldier conducted himself with courage and dignity. What else could they have said? Reno kept himself more or less together while men were being killed all around him. I don't see how anyone could have asked for more.

The Court of Inquiry's verdict, like Benteen's, damned Reno with faint praise. He may not have been a brilliant commander, they held, but none of his actions merited censure. Even that didn't matter in the long run. The court's finding was only a mundane fact, swept aside by Libbie Custer's campaign to romanticize her husband, and even more, I think, by our cultural need for heroes and myths around the Euro- American westward expansion. Reno eventually died in poverty, alone and despised. Custer became the gallant hero of western legend. His reputation held firm until the cultural re-examinations of the 1960s.

PARANOIA UNDER THE GROUND

I've been reading about Custer, Reno, and Benteen ever since I was a child growing up in western Colorado. As I drove through Wyoming and into Montana, I had plenty of time to think about how each of them "assumed worst intentions" about the others. I had plenty of time to mix and match Custer with what I had seen at the Minuteman Missile National Historic Site, and from online and written sources I've perused. There's a lot of paranoia out there, and it can be deadly.

Back in South Dakota I had stared down at a replica missile, mute in its silo dug into the prairie. The silo cover had been rolled back, replaced with a thick plexiglass lens, so I could look down at the weapon itself. It looked deceptively lithe and graceful, the sleek nosecone small enough to fit in the back of my car. But it contained three independently targeted warheads, each one fifty times as powerful as the bomb that destroyed Nagasaki. Custer, Reno, and Benteen assumed worst intentions and it caused plenty of tragedy. But in that fight, the most powerful weapon was a rifle.

Ah, paranoia: people assuming worst intentions, fearful

of others' power to carry them out. The focal point of the launch control center I toured was that red steel box with the padlocks on it. White letters were stenciled on each side, "ENTRY RESTRICTED TO MISSILE COMBAT CREW COMMANDER AND DEPUTY MISSILE COMBAT CREW COMMANDER ON DUTY."

At the end of each twenty-four-hour watch, the two departing officers would take their padlocks off the red box. Two oncoming officers would put theirs on. The only other time they would remove their locks was if they received orders to actually open the box.

I would hate to serve a twenty-four-hour watch amid those switches and indicator lights in a concrete submarine buried four stories underground. They had television to relieve the boredom. They had telephones to talk with other launch control centers or anywhere else they wanted. Just to talk to friends or loved ones through the boring hours. I don't think I could talk enough to do that job.

Old military artifacts present an air of impregnability, be they medieval castles, a Revolutionary War fortress, battleships, or ballistic missile control centers. Weapons and fortifications always look so damned strong, how could anything possibly go wrong?

Yet castles got besieged and sacked. Fortresses got overrun. Battleships got torpedoed and sunk. Up at Wounded Knee, three hundred Lakota were gunned down, basically, for dancing. Miscalculation seems to be the common human lot. Add to that a lethal dismissal of "the other's" humanity, and "the fog of war" gets deadly.

Uranium enrichment seemed a triumph of the good during the Second World War and for years after. Working on Little Boy and Fat Man, J. Robert Oppenheimer and his team focused on the technology. The prospect of American and Soviet nuclear triads, glaring at one another from opposite sides of the world, was outside the circle of their vision.

Once Oppenheimer's "gadgets" destroyed two hundred thousand or so people, he developed misgivings. But post-World War II rivalries had an energy all their own. Oppenheimer warned anyone who would listen about nuclear proliferation. The only result was to lose his own security clearance in the rush toward Mutual Assured Destruction.

I watched one online video, a former missile launch commander telling his own story of paranoia and the fog of war. November 9, 1979, alarms went off in launch control centers across the American Midwest. Printers rattled out commands and confirmation numbers, ordering launch control officers to open their launch key boxes.

The officer telling this story, and his partner, took their padlocks off. They took out the envelope with the matching confirmation code and the two innocent-looking keys. They went through the checklist of launch preparations, then inserted their launch keys into their switches.

The officer telling this story began to tear up. They had never gone this far with a drill. They were now waiting for the final order, a point they would reach only if they faced a full nuclear exchange. Minutes ticked by. While they waited, he used the outside landline to call his wife. Of course he couldn't breathe a syllable of what was going on. He tried to sound nonchalant and asked her if there was anything interesting on the news. Looking for a hint of why he had his trigger finger on thirty megatons of nuclear warheads. His wife replied, no, there wasn't any interesting news.

They talked for a few minutes. He finally bade her goodbye and hung up the phone. The man said he believed he would never hear his wife's voice again.

Finally, to his trembling relief and, one presumes, the relief of launch officers from North Dakota down to

Arkansas, the next order was to "stand down." They were told to remove launch keys, return them to the red boxes, and shut down launch systems.

They would later find out that surveillance computers had, in fact, indicated a full missile launch by the Soviet Union. Air Defense command had scrambled airplanes. The President's "doomsday plane" had taken off. But early warning satellites failed to confirm a Soviet launch. After hesitation and frantic conferring, NORAD's command declined to respond.

Someone, it later turned out, had inserted the wrong training tape into the air defense computer system. A mistaken training tape—that's all it was—had triggered alarms and put keys into launch switches across the American Midwest. Thirty years later, this former launch officer finished telling his story. He sat down. He was, as witnesses put it, "quite emotional." I'd be emotional too.

SEPTEMBER 1, 1983

*W*e measure the stars. We peer into the intimacies of the atom. We extract the puissant essence of uranium and make it our slave. It provides us with electrical power, beams neutrons at cancer cells, or if we are "provoked," launches weapons that will destroy multitudes. Damn, we're good. But behind and below the frontal lobes of our brains, we rely on the same neural equipment as an alligator chomping a muskrat.

It never occurred to me, going through that ballistic missile site on my standard four-times-a-day public tour, that we were being watched. Only later was I reminded, Soviet and American spy satellites have optics that can view that preserved missile in its silo, watch me drive, even read the license plate on my car. Such "eyes-in-the-sky" have been orbiting for decades. They're marvels of technology, those satellites, but they have their glitches, same as we have ours. The minds that design and operate them are as vulnerable to assumed worst intentions as Custer, Reno, and Benteen, snarling at one another in the hills above the Little Bighorn.

The "training-tape" story gave me the willies. It also set

me to wider exploration. During a five-year period, the two great powers came within a cat's whisker of a nuclear exchange—repeatedly. There were also hundreds of "broken arrow" nuclear weapons accidents on both sides of the Atlantic, some of which were reported but many of which were not. Such things didn't make headlines. Even national leaders didn't always know the details.

I did read headlines in 1983 about the Russian shoot-down of a commercial passenger jet over the Pacific Ocean. That happened thousands of miles west of that missile control center I visited. Delving more deeply, though, I learned that tragedy began with a surveillance satellite similar to the one eyeballing us tourists on our missile site tour.

September 1, 1983, a Soviet satellite was watching an American Boeing RC-135 military surveillance airplane. It was flying figure-8s off the coast of the Soviet Union's Kamchatka Peninsula. *The image drills into my mind, the RC-135, the figure-8s, the cat-and-mouse game played on both sides. Kamchatka is a sensitive place. The Soviets plan to test launch a new missile there the next morning, which is why the RC-135 is gathering all the data it can. It's watching the Soviets while their satellite watches it, all part of the endless game. Our spy planes have even breached Soviet airspace a few times. But such games get people killed.*

I have memories from my own, long-ago military service: dim, red lights, green radar displays, projected tracks on combat information maneuvering boards. *That feeds my image of hard, stern Soviet officers who study complex displays. They also track blips flying along a nearby commercial air traffic corridor. This part of the Pacific is busy with passenger flights. One commercial blip slowly veers out of the corridor and merges with the RC-135 blip. In the Soviet command center, officers don't pay much attention until the blip heads into Soviet airspace. They stare* in disbelief, then scramble fighter planes. By the time the fighter planes climb to altitude, though, the blip has crossed the Kamchatka Peninsula and is back out over international waters.

Frustrated, officers keep an intense watch. The blip heads straight toward Sakhalin Island, another sensitive area. It's crucial to Soviet oil production and security facilities. Officers scowl and raise their voices. This harassment is beyond all proper bounds. Again, they scramble fighters. This time the Soviet fighter pilot makes visual contact, reporting that it's a large plane, brightly lit. Size is right for a RC-135.

The pilot tries to contact it, using all known American military frequencies. No response. Ground command orders him to fire a machine gun burst past it. They assume the fighter has phosphorus-treated tracer rounds, which light up brightly. Designed to help accuracy, the bright tracers will get the attention of the suspect airplane's pilot. If he doesn't respond to that, he's definitely up to no good.

But there have been crucial misunderstandings. First, ground command doesn't know the inefficient Soviet supply system has not delivered tracer ammunition to this fighter wing for six months. Their fighter is armed only with standard rounds. The pilot can shoot all he wants, but the mystery plane will never notice. Second, it has not occurred to the pilot or ground command, either one, to try hailing the suspect plane on any commercial frequency.

The pilot fires a machine gun burst. The mystery plane continues to ignore him. Missing that crucial detail, the missing tracer rounds, ground command instructs him to arm an air-to-air missile and shoot the intruder down. A few seconds later, the pilot reports, "Target destroyed."

So perishes Korean Air Lines (KAL) Flight 007, carrying two hundred sixty-seven civilians. Due to pilot error and a technical malfunction, no one on the plane realized they were two hundred miles off course. Meanwhile, America's RC-135 spy plane lands, unremarked, at its base in Alaska.

Human error and paranoia. It's a bad combination. I grew up marinated in standard Euro-American assumptions about the Soviet Union. I was, therefore, madder than hell when KAL 007 got shot down. Paranoia.

President Ronald Reagan went on television and called the Soviet Union "the evil empire" and a nation of "barbarians." How could any civilized nation shoot down a commercial airliner full of innocent civilians? At that time, I never dreamed of the story behind the story.

The Soviets blustered that KAL 007 was a spy plane. They partly believed that themselves, or at least that it was intentional provocation by the West. Paranoia.

The Soviet term for what *they* thought *we* were doing, is *maskarovka*. "Masking." That is, all that we publicly said or did was a mask for a deeper plan. Having witnessed the elections of 2016, I surmise the Russians of today know just as much about *maskarovka* as the old Soviets did, and are no less willing and able to practice it themselves than the old Soviet Union was. If Soviet leadership describe themselves as suspicious innocents, then or now, we know better. But that's the point of paranoia. We who practice to deceive—are also scared to death the "other guy" is doing it to us.

A century and a half earlier, Marcus Reno and Frederick Benteen feared that Custer had left them to die. They didn't think twice that they were doing that very same thing to Custer.

It's easy to see the Russians in their twenty-first century *maskarovka,* their interference in Western elections. We'll be investigating and sorting that out for years. But it would be naïve to expect us to be as diligent—or as outraged—when we do it ourselves.

SEPTEMBER 26, 1983

*L*ess than a month after the shoot-down of KAL Flight 007, Lieutenant Colonel Stanislav Petrov goes on watch at the Soviet early-warning command center outside Moscow. His job is to monitor those Soviet surveillance satellites that watch tourists in the American Midwest and passenger flights across the Pacific.

Though just a mid-level officer, Petrov reports to the top of the Soviet hierarchy. He is, therefore, highly accountable. He would be the first to see a United States missile launch. The High Command will critique his every move. There's a certain boredom to this work, constantly watching. Also intense vulnerability.

A few hours into this shift, alarms suddenly blare. Red lights flash. On the white view screen in front of Petrov, huge, red letters say:

MISSILE LAUNCH.

The Soviet satellite which eyes our midwestern Minuteman missile silos has reported a launch. Petrov starts from his chair. He goes through his confirmation checklist. This is a new system. It would be easy for him to miss some nuance of operation. But the satellite is functioning properly.

He examines the visual feed and sees, as he will later describe, "points of light sparkling all over the place." Across the lands where Crow, Oyate, and Cheyenne used to hunt buffalo—beneath which the US military have hidden thousands of nuclear warheads—bright sparks flash. If missiles were rising from those silos, though, there should be telltale white exhaust tracks. Petrov doesn't see that. Interpreting the information as best he can, he silences the alarm.

Less than a minute passes. Then alarms blare, lights flash, and the big screen lights up again:

MISSILE LAUNCH.

This is deadly serious. This time, as Petrov goes back through the equipment checklist, the system automatically informs his commanding officer. The desk telephone jangles and the commander demands to know what's going on. Despite the light flashes on visual, Petrov still sees no missile tracks. He tells the officer this, and that he is disabling the system again. Once more, it's quiet.

He barely has time to set the phone receiver back onto its cradle when it happens again, the flashing lights, the alarm louder and more insistent than ever. This time, the display changes to:

MISSILE ATTACK.

On this third warning, the system automatically notifies top Soviet leadership. Soviet Premier Yuri Andropov is an old man in hospital, dying from renal failure. On his last legs, he is deeply suspicious of the United States. The command comes down from the very top for confirmation on the launch. They have less than ten minutes to decide on a full nuclear response.

Petrov is drenched in his own sweat. "I started feeling like I was sitting in a hot frying pan," he would later say. "I couldn't feel my feet." The Soviet command will hold him responsible for the nation's fate. If one American missile enters Soviet air space before Petrov has authorized a launch, he knows his remaining days will be few and miserable.

Sweat soaks Petrov's uniform and drips down the small of his back. He can only rely on his training. The sun is setting across the midwestern United States, lengthening shadows, making visibility terrible. According to the satellite, five American missiles have launched and are on their way. But he still sees no missile tracks on visual. He stubbornly hangs on in the face of the pressure, looking for something definite by which to judge.

Twice more, the alarms go off. The telephone voices become more frantic. Against repeated electronic alarms, Petrov has only his training, his human understanding of the system, and intuition of how his fellow human beings on the other side of the ocean might really act. There are no rising missile tracks. But what if the Americans have designed some fiendish way to mask nuclear missile exhaust?

Still, he tells himself, the launch of five American missiles doesn't make sense. Even if every warhead hit its target, a mere five missiles could not hope to take out Soviet response capability. An American nuclear attack would be a massive launch: all their missiles.

It doesn't make sense, he tells himself again. Despite alarms, ringing telephones, and demands for confirmation, he holds fast.

Then—nothing. The alarms go silent. The visual spots of light fade and die away. North America goes dark. Later, investigation will reveal a design flaw in the new satellite monitoring system. Under the right conditions, light from the setting sun can bounce off high clouds over the United States and into the satellites' infrared sensors. This is what triggered the multiple launch alarms.

Petrov finishes out the night's watch, bathed in sweat, shivering with relief. He goes home to his wife after the shift is over, more glad to see her than he has ever been in his life. They embrace and she asks him, "So what did you to tonight?" "Nothing," he replies. "I did nothing."

He doesn't sleep that night or the night after. Later, he will be diagnosed with post-traumatic stress disorder.

*A*lthough those launch warnings turned out to be satellite glitches, respite from nuclear tension is short. The United States and North Atlantic Treaty Organization (NATO) know nothing about the Soviet nuclear panic. Themselves paranoid about Soviet intentions, they continue to escalate.

In the United States, President Ronald Reagan believes the best policy for peace is strength in the face of Soviet "aggression." Reagan supports research on new missile defense systems, as well as stationing new American Pershing II mid-range nuclear missiles in Europe. This puts American nuclear warheads just a few hundred miles from Soviet air space.

Two months after the KAL 007 shoot-down, one month after the Soviet missile defense scare, Reagan authorizes a massive command communications drill with NATO. It's called Operation Able Archer. It will simulate an escalating world-wide crisis, to end with a simulated nuclear launch. For a week, the exercise will simulate all the messaging of a run-up to nuclear war.

Messages are coded, so Soviet surveillance cannot read them. The Soviets can monitor the communication networks and patterns, though, and they are disturbing. Radio messages buzz between NATO bases all across Western Europe and North America.

Each message has a plain-text preface: "TrainingExercise!TrainingExercise!TrainingExercise!"

This only makes Soviet monitors more suspicious. They practice maskarovka. They therefore assume that we practice maskarovka. The very words, "TrainingExercise," raise suspicions that this is not a real training exercise, but a deadly threat. In Soviet minds, only one country has actually used nuclear weapons in war: the United States. Given Reagan's rhetoric, what better way to gain surprise than by masking it as a training exercise?

Paranoia. The Soviets still suspect we tricked them into downing KAL 007. Will that be our excuse for a massive launch? What's really behind this intense message traffic? With Premier Andropov in the hospital, Soviet leadership is frantic not to get caught napping.

Paranoia.

Across Washington and Europe, the communications exercise escalates. Listening in, the Soviets put their own nuclear arsenal on hair-trigger alert. They disburse SS-20 mobile nuclear missile launchers into the field, armed and ready.

Operation Able Archer proceeds according to script. In Premier Andropov's hospital room and at Soviet military headquarters, those in high command send out their launch codes. They open their launch authorization briefcases.

Through the night, November 8, 1983, Soviet fingers rest on nuclear triggers. On America's side of the Atlantic, we know we're the "good guys." Surely, everyone else knows we're the "good guys." No one in the White House dreams that the Soviet Union could consider us anything other than harmless "good guys."

At dawn on November 9, the Soviets intercept an American signal that nuclear missiles have been launched. American targets are keyed into Soviet launch computers awaiting final, last-second *confirmation. Minutes tick by. Early warning command waits only for tell-tale tracks of American missiles rising from their silos.*

Then—again—nothing. Operation Able Archer '83 ends on schedule. Across America and Europe, command personnel congratulate themselves on a job well done. They relax and go home to celebrate Veterans' Day. Across the Soviet Union, military high command personnel mop the sweat off their brows and wonder:

How could those Americans be so irresponsible?

Maskarovka. A generation later, top Russian leaders, who were junior officers during the Operation Able Archer nightmare, will approve Russian interference with the United States' presidential election process. There is no sign that they note the irony.

I read such accounts with fascination, sadness, also fear. There are any number of mishaps, sudden or gradual, which would paralyze the way of life we take for granted. In which corner of our future does our cultural devastation lurk? Who holds the leash? If it's the dominant culture itself that holds the leash, does that make it less inevitable? Or just more ironic?

PART V
RADICAL HOPE

Once you are dead . . . all the differences of this world are not important.

—architect John Collins, on his design for the Little Bighorn Battlefield Indian Memorial

AFTERMATH

*F*or months after my rolling spiritual retreat, search terms such as "Stanislav Petrov," "training tape incident," "KAL 007, and "Operation Able Archer" drew me down their branching internet byways. We've had our toes on the threshold of Armageddon plenty of times. One more equipment glitch or mental hiccup and we'd have entered an era better measured by science fiction writers than scientists.

We owe a debt of thanks to Stanislav Petrov. Caught between unforgiving superiors and screaming technology, he fell back on his sense of commonality with us, the enemy. He banked that Americans would act the same as humans he knew on his side of the Atlantic. If he had been a little less trained or a little less balanced, would further fail-safe measures down the line have prevented an all-out exchange?

Petrov received praise at first. But high-ranking officers were invested in their new warning system. Too much discussion of system flaws might embarrass the wrong people. So they hushed up the incident and secretly worked out the problems. Petrov found himself shunted to an obscure, dead-end duty station. "The bird sitting on the higher branch shits on the bird that's on the lower branch," he later observed. Later, he suffered a nervous breakdown. I observe that sometimes a nervous breakdown is the mark of a sane human being in an insane situation. Major Reno might understand.

When the Soviet Union collapsed, the story got out. Petrov finally received due honor. A Danish company made a documentary about him, *The Man Who Saved the World*. He was even brought to America and got to meet actor Kevin Costner. But his close call was just one of the many which could have altered our world forever.

In 1983, according to informed sources, the only people who really understood how near the brink we were, were the spies. Only after America's Central Intelligence Agency (CIA) compared notes between Able Archer leadership and foreign spy networks, did they realize the nightmare peeking over their shoulders. They were dismayed.

Former CIA Director and Defense Secretary, Robert Gates, has said, "The most terrifying thing about Able Archer was that we may have been at the brink of nuclear war *and not even known it*." The CIA informed the White House of this. President Ronald Reagan never read reports, but he had just watched a television drama about nuclear Armageddon titled, *The Day After*.

In what even an atheist might call divine coincidence, *The Day After* aired just a couple weeks after Operation Able Archer. It left Reagan depressed, staffers said. When they told him it had nearly happened for real, he was, they say, "very moved."

Soviet Premier Yuri Andropov soon died. So did his successor, Konstantin Chernenko. Then came Mikhail Gorbachev. One thing led to another, ice broke, relations thawed a bit. In 1988, Reagan, who had called the Soviet

Union "barbarians" and "the evil empire," visited Gorbachev in Moscow. During a dual press event, a reporter asked Reagan, "Do you still think that we're an evil empire, Mr. President?"

There was a long silence. Then Reagan put his arm around Gorbachev's shoulder and said, "No." That's something, at least. "The other guy" is human, too. We don't always have to be paranoid, after all. But it wasn't the last time we came within a gnat's eyelash of blasting one another.

A generation later we seem to be stepping back into times Reagan might find "very moving." Warheads still lurk beneath the plains, in the air, in the sea. Culture dances to quick-times piped by evolving technology and ongoing paranoia. It would be hubris to tell ourselves we control that technology or even ourselves.

I conjure Plenty Coups's aged face in 1930, commenting on the way white folks can fool themselves. All folks, really. We're all "good guys" in our own eyes: Sitting Bull, Crazy Horse, Custer, Reno, Benteen, the soldiers setting up their Hotchkiss guns at Wounded Knee. The "missileers" sliding keys into their launch switches.

Here's where this goes for me: the world we know right now is not the world we will always know. Our way of life may get knocked off the table by the earth's moods, by our own collective actions, or by some force we don't even yet foresee. But it will, sooner or later, get knocked off the table. When that happens, we will play by new rules. We will learn who we really are, if we can learn anything. But I doubt we'll like it any more than Pretty Shield and Plenty Coups liked it when Euro-Americans killed the last buffalo, put their people on the reservation, and their hearts "fell to the ground."

It occurs to me that Western culture plays by rules and

assumptions dating back to *Genesis*'s injunction to subdue the earth and have dominion over it. The less we question those assumptions, the closer we step to Half-Yellow-Face's "road we do not know."

In his book, *Radical Hope,* philosopher Jonathan Lear does a deep study of the Crow's response to their cultural collapse. For them, the catalyst was Euro-American expansion. For the dominant culture, who knows? But the present balances fine before the windy eons, and the social and physical forces that blow from beyond our ken. No center, I say, holds forever.

UTES

I grew up in the mid-twentieth century, first in Colorado, then in Utah. I spent most of my life within spitting distance of Native American history, but thought little about it. Never had to. I have been told that's precisely what "white privilege" is. It didn't occur to me, till decades later, how blind I was to indigenous issues even as I walked land and drank water that was theirs during my great-grandfather's lifetime.

We don't even have a common and respectful word for our indigenous neighbors. "Indians" is, of course, incorrect. Grade school kids learn that. But, some indigenous people tell me, "Amerindians" and "Native Americans" don't go down much better with them. Their ancestors were here thousands of years before the place became America.

Naming the people my forbears swept aside is, to me, an issue with which the dominant culture needs to struggle. I certainly do. Not least because they were not singular. They were hundreds of nations, thousands of clans, spanning two continents.

Most Indians-Native Americans-First Nations accept

white carelessness. They haven't had much choice. That is, I gather, one small piece of the practice of survivance. A person outside the dominant culture needs a sense of irony and humor to navigate the constant slights, stereotypes, and blithe ignorance. Expand that to our entire culture, throw in African, Asian, Latino, BGLTQ folk, and to a large extent women, and we begin to get a sense of the exhausting ocean of dances a straight, blue-eyed, good old boy, such as myself, does *not* have to do.

I was born in Grand Junction, Colorado, fifty miles east of the Utah-Colorado line. Most towns in western Colorado were founded within a couple years of one another, dating to the expulsion of Colorado's indigenous Ute people. The Utes gone in September 1881, and bang! White settlers flooding in, towns springing up before Ute tears had even dried on their footprints. In my childhood Grand Junction's oldest residents could still recall the Utes's expulsion and the town's founding. Yet I never connected the two until long after I reached adulthood.

The Utes would know how the Lakota felt about the Black Hills. Ute territory spanned eastern Utah, western Colorado, and northern New Mexico. Then the boom got lowered, and by 1882 they found themselves confined to a patchwork of desert and plateau in Utah and southernmost Colorado. Not much grows there. Mountain Utes became Desert Utes with a swipe of pen on paper.

As teenagers in Utah, some friends and I once drove to reservation headquarters in Fort Duchesne to buy deer hunting permits. In those years Ute tribal land offered the best deer hunting in the state.

I remember thinking to myself, the weathered Ute man who filled out my paperwork and took my payment didn't act very friendly. My friends and I were laughing and joking, excited about the potential of bagging nice bucks. He sat there dour faced, his pen working its way down the form he was filling out for us.

Only years later did it occur to me, of *course* he hadn't been friendly. The poverty rate on that reservation was over 50 percent. It still is. They sold hunting rights to white folks like me precisely because they needed the money. After all, said white folks like me had taken away all the land fertile enough to provide a living.

Like a lot of Euro-Americans, I squirmed reading African American journalist Ta-Nehisi Coates's declaration that "white American progress is built on looting and violence." The media grilled him for that claim. But looking over my own shoulder, I can't deny it's my heritage.

Here's how my piece of that heritage worked. Reading up on Ute Chief Ouray, I learned that he died before enough Utes had signed to ratify the 1880 treaty which drastically reduced their reservation. (As a sick old man, he only supported it because he feared the army would annihilate the Utes if he didn't.) His death left federal Ute agent, Otto Mears, a thousand signatures short of the number he needed.

No problem. Mears set about bribing the grieving Ute tribal elders: two dollars a signature, a nice sum in 1880. He didn't bother to provide details on what their signatures meant. The treaty called for the Northern Utes to be resettled in western Colorado's Grand Valley. Violating even those terms, Mears and the army instead moved them far northwest, to the arid canyons and cliffs of eastern Utah. On the grounds, he said, the Grand Valley was "not fertile enough for farming."

Grand Junction sprang up there a couple years later. I was born sixty-eight years after that. I grew up amid the Grand Valley's sugar beet fields, cattle and poultry ranches, and so many apricot and peach orchards, we called it, "Colorado's Fruit Basket." I wasn't there while Otto Mears was applying his entrepreneurial skills, of course. But his deceit allowed me to be born there.

I know what the Native American genocide tastes like. In western Colorado, at least. It tastes like peaches.

I grew up amid place names of indigenous eradication: Arapahoe, Apache, Blackfeet, Kiowa, Paiute, Shoshone, Ute. Yes, I was sympathetic. Sort of. But only when I thought about it, which was hardly ever. We whites had to kill Crazy Horse before we could market him.

But given another century, with more of this world's anthropocentric changes, will our culture feel any more fortunate than indigenous cultures felt as Euro-Americans pressed them flat? I don't think so. Our way of life is not sustainable. Plenty Coups and Pretty Shield were not "the old guard." They were prophets.

BATTLEFIELD

I touched Crazy Horse's death marker at Fort Robinson. I drove the ridges where the army cornered Dull Knife's fleeing Cheyenne warriors. I inhaled the air of Wounded Knee. How could my route not curve toward the Crow Reservation and Little Bighorn Battlefield National Monument? The Cheyenne and Lakota got their revenge there, but it was costly satisfaction.

As I crossed the state line into Montana, the high prairie humped into higher ridges and drier valleys. Before I realized it, I had crossed a divide into a picturesque valley artificially greened by wheel-line irrigation. A silver ribbon to my right wound through goose necks and sandbars. That, I learned at the next bridge, was the Little Bighorn River. Cottonwood groves towered above the waters, wide leaves that rattle in a breeze. Above them loomed hilltops pale with sagebrush and September prairie grass.

Swinging off onto the national monument exit, I was surprised at the steep climb up from the valley floor. The land was deceptive. It looked congenially flat from a distance, but the ridge tops were cut up as hell. No wonder

Custer's horses and men were worn out and Major Reno's survivors went near-crazy with thirst.

I had been the only one around when I visited Wounded Knee. No visitor center, no museum, no park rangers reciting the event's history to enthralled crowds. Little Bighorn National Monument was a different matter entirely. It was full of tourists. Cars, minivans, and monster motor homes jammed the vast parking lot.

I parked my car and found myself looking down on the Custer National Military Cemetery. A well-sprinkled lawn, artificially green against the pervasive dun, sloped away toward the river and the valley beyond that. Pine trees stood sentry over row on precise row of military headstones, a petrified march down the hillside.

A brochure informed me that the men killed with Custer were buried where they lay, shallow and hasty. I'd be hasty, too, handling mutilated corpses that had lain out in the summer sun for two days. The bones weathered back out of the ground within months, scattered by scavengers, broken, and disbursed. Prodded by concerned citizens, the army sent details to rebury what bones they could find in 1877, 1879, and 1881.

They added headstones in 1890, going by records from the first burial detail. Some bodies were later interred in a mass grave below the granite obelisk that marks where Custer fell. Others were moved to the cemetery, which later expanded to five thousand graves, joining Arlington and West Point as official Armed Forces memorials. Veterans of many American wars now lie here. So do five of Custer's six Crow scouts.

I joined tourists walking up the ridge toward the Custer Monument. A pale, granite spire, it looks down from the battlefield's highest point. I later learned this was an "American" monument, that is, a *white* American monument. It may lie on Crow Reservation land, but Custer's legend was really about the cost and glory of Manifest Destiny. Indigenous people need not apply.

Message sent. As far as indigenous Americans were concerned, message definitely received. First Nation victory though it was, I read that few of them would visit the Monument. Except, sometimes Crow boys would sneak up to the obelisk, tap it with sticks, then run away giggling. "Counting coup," don't you see?

I couldn't miss the glum-looking, white headstones scattered through the prairie grass. This was, I read, the only battlefield on earth that marks where the individual soldiers fell. Well—from one side, anyway. The Lakota and Cheyenne carried their dead away and consigned them according to traditional practice.

About three dozen headstones clustered within a low, wrought-iron enclosure right below the spire. For generations that fence marked Custer's gallant "last stand." That was before archeology and First Nation descriptions of the battle confirmed there never was a last stand. As Captain Benteen had summed it up on the witness stand, it had been "a complete rout." Most of Custer's command was already dead, bodies scattered along a mile of ridge tops, before he and his last thirty-odd men wound up there.

The air was high, dry and hot. People moved quietly. They spoke in subdued voices, if they talked at all. Almost everyone seemed respectful before these unmistakable markers of violent mortality.

PEACE THROUGH UNITY

*A*s I drew close to the obelisk dedicated to Custer, an incongruent roundness came into view above the hill's far slope. It drew my eyes. Atop a low earthen dome, framed against the sky, loomed three striking wrought-iron outlines of mounted Native warriors. The sculptor, I later read, was Colleen Cutschall, a Lakota woman born on Pine Ridge Reservation. She titled it *Spirit Warriors*.

This was the new Indian Memorial. The lengthy process by which it came about teaches something about the silent message of this place. Silent messages are only silent until you challenge them. Then they bellow like a bull being tortured.

Through the cultural introspection of the 1960s and the American Indian Movement a decade later, impetus grew to honor both sides on this battlefield. That touched off instant controversy. Opponents claimed that a memorial to First Nations would somehow "Indianize" the battlefield. One editorial protested it would be like "building a memorial to the Mexicans killed at the Alamo."

Considering that "Indians" won this battle, and that this

monument was carved out of "Indian" land—and far as that goes, that San Antonio was part of Mexico when the Alamo fight took place—that would be a bad idea, why?

It's not lost on me that Boston-born Korczak Ziolkowski could carve a cyclopean, generic figure of an "Indian" in the sacred Black Hills, call it "Crazy Horse," and it's a million dollar tourist attraction. But a monument to the warriors who routed Custer, designed by those warriors' descendants —is controversial? I'll just let that sit there.

Below the *Spirit Warriors* installation, a concrete walkway wound down to a sunken court. Granite plaques honored the First Nations who fought there. On both sides. Crow and Arikara men scouted for Custer. Lakota, Yanktonai, Santee, Northern Cheyenne, Arapahoe battled him. Each Nation got its own plaque. It didn't look to me as though the women and children killed by Major Reno's initial attack were among the dozens of names listed, but I could be wrong.

Like Cutchall, the memorial's architect, John Collins, is also of indigenous descent. In his notes, he comments that he designed the memorial as a circle because the circle is a sacred shape to Great Plains Nations. To me, the design evokes their reality another way. Above, striking though the wrought iron installation was, it presented the stereotype: mounted warriors in familiar guise; below, I found myself in a richer, more nuanced world, hidden until I was in the middle of it.

A stone-lined notch on one side opened toward Custer's obelisk. Collins calls the notch and the stone "Weeping Walls" on both sides of the notch, "a link between the two [monuments] welcoming the dead so there can be an exchange of spirits." He goes on to say, "Once you are dead, . . . you have a better understanding of the infinite from where you came. All the differences of this world are not important."

"Once you are dead, all the differences of this world are not important." I jotted that down in my notebook.

A trickle of water ran along the bottom of the notch to a pool in the center of the circle. Meant, I read, to symbolize the Weeping Wall's tears. It didn't specify for whom to weep, a metaphor I interpret in the largest sense.

Looking up through the notch, I did feel the presence of complex human themes. The 7th Cavalry monument is a Victorian-era memorial to America's expansionist past, the noble dead lost in pursuit of empire. Soldiers perished and were buried where they fell, now marked by those scattered headstones.

The 7th Cavalry had dozens of First Nation scouts, so the Indian Memorial is not just an afterthought on behalf of battle's victors. It's deeper than that—a paean to indigenous allies, as well, crushed but resilient against Manifest Destiny.

The *New York Times* wrote that Little Bighorn National Monument "is the nation's most polarized park." I saw Wounded Knee as a monument to the heartbreaking indigenous struggle against Euro-American conquest. Looking back at Custer, Benteen, Reno, their paranoia and loathing for one another, and Custer's disdain for the Crow scouts who tried to warn him, perhaps the Little Bighorn Battlefield is a monument to something just as poignant: the heartbreaking things we can do to ourselves.

WHITE SWAN

*E*very Crow who mentioned the six Crow scouts with Custer spoke of them with pride. Unlike Custer, they all survived to live long lives. They knew this country like the backs of their hands, but they had only been with Custer a week or so. He didn't trust any "Indian" he didn't know well. He therefore considered them of no use. Ironically, when he sent them packing, he saved their lives.

From a distant hilltop, four of them watched Custer lead his men down Medicine Tail Coulee, a long, broad valley toward the river. Seeing the clouds of disaster gather, they rode home with early tidings that Custer was going to have a bad day.

The two others rode with Major Reno as he attacked the south end of the camp. One was the Crow scouts' leader, or "shirt-wearer," Half-Yellow-Face. The other was a good natured young man called White Swan. White Swan fell at the river's edge, shot in ankle and wrist, his forehead bashed in by a Lakota war club.

He would have died then and there, had not Half-Yellow-

Face dragged him to a brushy hiding place as the fighting moved up a gully and away from the river. Half-Yellow-Face also saved six white soldiers the same way. Once things settled a bit, he managed to lead them all up to where Reno's survivors had dug in atop the bluff.

Between 1878 and 1895, Congress handed out twenty-four Medals of Honor for heroism at the Little Big Horn. Half-Yellow-Face's deeds matched the best of them, but he was left off the heroes list. Medals of Honor were for white soldiers, not "Indians."

After a two-day siege, Reno's exhausted men watched the Lakota and Cheyenne decamp and depart, a massive human river flowing south toward the Bighorn Mountains. General Alfred Terry's infantry marched in from the opposite direction later that afternoon. Thus relieved, the remnant of the 7th Cavalry set about binding wounds and burying their dead.

White Swan could not walk. There was doubt whether he would survive at all. Resorting to traditional Crow transportation, Half-Yellow-Face built him a horse-drawn travois. White Swan made the journey to base camp on the Yellowstone River in relative comfort, gently undulating as the horse dragged those limber limbs over brush and rock.

Believing Half-Yellow-Face had nothing to teach them on handling the wounded, soldiers rigged mule-back litters to transport their casualties. Because mules move and behave— well, like mules—that turned into a study in misery. It was a jostling ride at best. Some litters fell off. One mule decided to stop and sit on its haunches, rolling its passenger, a wounded sergeant, off on the ground. Soldiers later commented on the man's fortitude, keeping stoic silence through his agony.

At a temporary field hospital, army surgeons saved White Swan's life. He limped for the rest of his days, and his right hand healed badly from the bullet through his wrist. Due to brain damage from the war club, he never spoke again. Even so, as soon as he was up and around, he resumed scouting for the army. He used Crow sign language to communicate.

A year after the battle, the army built Fort Custer a few miles from Last Stand Hill. Crow Agency, the focal point of the new Crow Reservation, sprang up nearby. When White Swan finally retired on a tiny army pension, Crow Agency was where he settled. He became a favorite with soldiers and tourists, sometimes posing for photographs. They show a pleasant looking man, his face serene or perhaps just inscrutable. There's a visible dent in his forehead, where the war club struck, and his right hand is stiff and twisted from that wound. I can't imagine what his dreams must have been like.

In *Radical Hope*, Lear juxtaposes two types of courage, crucially different from one another. There's the warrior's resolve to "go down fighting," as Lear puts it, embodied by the fearless-but-hopeless defiance of Crazy Horse and Sitting Bull. And, perhaps, by the arrogant courage of Custer.

There's also a more complex form, the resolve to accept and proceed creatively, into a future so changed, there are no longer even words to describe it. That was the form the Crow elders adopted.

Like them, White Swan never seems to have given up on his white allies. It would have been understandable for him to surrender to despair, but he responded creatively as his physical strength waned. To supplement his meagre retirement, he took to painting Crow motifs onto paper or linen, selling them to tourists and travelers for what he could get. Some of his art still survives in museums and private collections. His courage—resilience—survivance—were prodigious.

The first superintendent's home at Custer Cemetery, a neat brick structure, became the White Swan Library in 1998, housing research archives and artifacts related to the battle. That strikes me as a fitting tribute to a remarkable life.

MAJOR RENO

*J*ust east of the White Swan Library, I happened
onto Major Reno's grave. I was glad to find him
there. Reno was not a great man, but he was a lot
better than Custer's fans have assessed him over the decades.
He was sent with one hundred ten men, a third of them raw
recruits, to charge thousands of warriors, many of whom
were better armed than his men were. It's hard to impress
under such circumstances.

Custer fans still blame Reno for Custer's demise. I find
that silly. It was four miles from Reno's defensive position to
Last Stand Hill, a valley swarming with Lakota and
Cheyenne armed to the teeth. Reno and Benteen could have
gotten themselves killed by venturing down there to look for
Custer. They could not have saved him.

Reno never recovered emotionally. The Army's Court of
Inquiry absolved him of blame, but he got in trouble two
years later for drunkenness and conduct unbecoming an
officer. He had, by then, pretty well fallen to pieces. He was
court-martialed, booted out of the army, and died poor,
buried in an unmarked grave in Washington, D. C. Over the

decades, there were proposals to set a stone for him at the Custer Cemetery. Each time, Custer's widow, Libbie, would campaign against it. As late as 1926, she implored the army "not to single out for honor, the one coward of the regiment."

By the 1960s, we had begun to learn more about shell shock, battle fatigue, and post-traumatic stress disorder, and that the wounded—physically or mentally—should not be punished for their suffering. The army, persuaded to revisit Reno's court- martial, finally reversed the verdict. They changed Reno's discharge to "honorable," located his remains, and re-buried him at Custer National Cemetery in 1967.

Custer's ambition took him to Last Stand Hill, surrounded by the noble dead. Reno was just a poor schmuck who tried to follow orders and found himself elbow deep in unanticipated trouble. The men who rode to their deaths with Custer would have been better off, had the glory-seeking Colonel been more like his mediocre subordinate.

This, I thought, standing over Reno's grave, is the human condition in small. Ultimate credit or blame, either one, doesn't mean much. Both get lost in a picture ever-so-much larger than we are, to be sorted out by later generations. If they're sorted out at all. "Once you are dead, all the differences of this world are not important." There are all kinds of battles: White Swan's battle, Custer's battle, Reno's battle. You wage your battle, I'll wage my battle. Judging is easy. The actual living is hard.

A SYMBOL

*I*ronically, because the soldiers' bones were exposed and re-buried and shifted and moved so many times, and because everyone wanted so badly to mark each man's fall, they wound up with about forty more markers than there were soldiers killed that day. As for Custer himself, soldiers sent to exhume his remains and send them to West Point for reburial couldn't find a grave to match the description they'd been given. In desperation, they dug up some bones they *hoped* were his and shipped them off. Later analysis indicates they're most likely not his. Not knowing that, Libbie Custer had herself buried beside them when she died in 1933.

Another slain officer was First Lieutenant James Sturgis. Friends called him "Jack." Firstborn of a military family, his father was General Sam Sturgis, who was technically Custer's commanding officer. Like many army officers, General Sturgis couldn't stand Custer, so the War Department kept them apart. As fate would have it, the son wound up in Custer's regiment.

Jack Sturgis was fresh out of West Point, youngest officer

in the command. Like a good third of Custer's men, he was one more "greenie." He was assigned to Company E. In the debacle at Custer's end of the battlefield, Company E is a particular mystery. The company commander's body was found with Custer on Last Stand Hill. The rest of the company's bodies have disappeared.

Going by the first burial record, as well as indigenous accounts of the battle, the best guess is that Company E panicked and fled on foot, down what's called Deep Ravine, toward the river. I stood below Custer's monument and gazed down that way. It would be a harrowing flight for men whom witnesses described as already wounded, limping along as best they could with warriors on the rim above them, attacking from all sides with rifles, bows, and war clubs. The image makes my skin crawl.

The first burial detail just caved the ravine's dirt walls in, covering the bodies where they lay. When later expeditions went to re-bury the bodies, they couldn't find them. No one had a clue where to put a marker for Jack Sturgis. So they didn't.

General Sturgis did not pass that detail to his grieving wife, Jerusha. To spare her feelings, he simply told her that Jack had been buried on the battlefield. Which was true as far as it went. A couple years passed. Fort Custer and Crow Agency sprang up a few miles from the battlefield, then Burlington Northern built a rail line through the valley. In 1878, Mrs. Sturgis declared her intention to travel to the battlefield and mourn at the grave of her firstborn.

This threw Fort Custer's soldiers into a panic. Not only did they not have a grave for Lieutenant Sturgis, they had no idea where to even put one. His bloody uniform had been found in the abandoned Lakota village. And—who would ever tell a mother this?—a burned head that might have been his. But the body? No one knew. How do you say such things to a mother, particularly when she's a general's wife?

With Mrs. Sturgis already en route, the soldiers did what they could. They gathered stones and piled them into a cairn in what seemed an apt place, up the slope from the river and within easy wagon access of Fort Custer. They made a marker from two boards and crudely lettered it across the top: "L' STURGIS—7th CAV JUNE '76."

It wasn't much, but the best they could do. Mrs. Sturgis arrived in the company of a detachment of soldiers led by Colonel Nelson Miles. They paid their military respects for her benefit. She spent her time at the "grave." Then they went back.

The cairn remained. To this day, Lieutenant Jack Sturgis' bones could be anywhere. They might possibly lie with the unknown enlisted men in the mass grave atop Last Stand Hill. He might be one of the twenty-eight remains counted in Deep Ravine, which cannot now be found. His bones might have been eroded out of the friable soil by rains, washed downhill into the Little Bighorn, and halfway down the Missouri River by now, headed for the eternal sea.

In 1904, the superintendent of Custer National Cemetery ordered a proper headstone for Lieutenant Jack Sturgis. He had it placed where Jerusha Sturgis had knelt to weep over her son.

I'm delighted that they did so. I see something properly and profoundly religious in the symbolism of Jack Sturgis' grave. It's not about the artifact, it's about what it means, what it allows the worshipper to give and receive. To me, Jack Sturgis' headstone is a tactile piece of the good work a religious symbol can do. A mother needed a myth, and it was pure kindness to provide one for her. If there's a living definition of such words as "spirituality" and "religion," to me, Jack Sturgis's rough stone cairn is what they look like.

You could take every memorial on Last Stand Hill, move it over a couple of ridge lines, re-establish the National Monument over there, and plow this one into cattle and alfalfa. The crowds would then drive over there. It would all still mean the same.

This is precisely why I, an atheist, have no problem whatsoever with traditional theistic religious worship. I believe the heart does need markers to help us clasp what's great and ultimate, and our own tininess in the face of it all. Americans, Christians, even skeptical Unitarian Universalists, all have myths to help us understand who we are.

I only ask that we mind the ways myth and reality can rub up against one another. There have to be ways to follow either and both to richer truth, deeper humility, love, compassion, enlightenment. While failure to do so causes us to wander from that which we truly seek. To me, a core religious task is to critically love both myth and reality for the discrete ways they can nurture and guide us. "Once you are dead . . . all the differences of this world are not important."

ARCHAEOLOGY

*B*ones still turn up here and there on the battlefield, found by tourists or archaeologists. So do other artifacts: bullets, casings, harness buckles, uniform buttons. Signs warn tourists not to use metal detectors or pick up artifacts. The battlefield is a shrine, not a prospecting site.

I saw other signs warning people to stay on sidewalks. This was rattlesnake country, they said, and I don't doubt it. I've encountered desert rattlers in such country, particularly south-facing slopes like this one. I also accept that, such is human nature, an ounce of real fear will make tourists behave better than a bushel of wise counsel.

Archaeologists have repeatedly analyzed the site. They've mapped where cartridge cases fell, where bullets struck, where bones and equipment were found, and what they looked like. They gradually got a sense of how the fight ran. The hard evidence agrees with First Nation accounts of the battle, which has surprised and offended some Custer devotees. Benteen was right, it was a rout. Myths can provide focus for our humanity. But we need to pay careful attention.

The Last Stand myth, I believe, was more about buoying up comfortable prejudices.

The recovered bones have been a forensic pathologist's dream. Custer's men were, on average, five-foot-seven in height. Some were pushing forty years old, but most were in their twenties. A few were still in their teens. Many suffered from bad teeth: untreated cavities, tobacco stains, wear from pipe stems. They had strong thighs from holding themselves on their horses, and bad backs from bouncing along on army saddles. Horses kick and buck, so there were many healed fractures. Some bones had bullet holes in them. Others show cut marks from being scalped or mutilated. Many skulls were shattered by what's called blunt force trauma. War clubs.

The 7th Cavalry was considered an elite force in 1876, but that puts a mighty low bar on "elite." Nutrition was poor. On the trail, the men lived on coffee, fried bacon, and hardtack so old you had to hit it with a rock to break it apart.

These soldiers were, in other words, just plain folks. A good third were foreign born. They came from Germany, Italy, the Low Countries, and the same place Tom McCarty did, Ireland. One presumes they came for the same reason my great-grandfather came, to make a new, better life. In other words, many of these men weren't really soldiers at all. They were farmers, barely trained or not at all for such deadly work.

But the United States was deep in recession back in 1876. Employment was hard to come by, the army needed men, so in they went. They didn't care about the ambitions of General Sheridan or Colonel Custer. They just wanted to make a living.

Some cases are particularly poignant. One was a skeleton recovered a half mile from a place called Weir Point. The distinguishing mark on this skeleton is a bullet hole through the right *ilium*, the flat bone of the hip. That, and the place it was found, clearly mark it as Company D's farrier, Private Vincent Charlie.

The farrier's job was part blacksmith, part veterinarian. Vincent Charlie cared for Company D's horses, shod them, trimmed their hooves. He was in his late twenties, and, at five-foot-ten, a strapping big kid by 7th Cavalry standards. One of his leg bones was broken and healed, as was one wrist, likely from horse kicks. His vertebrae show that like the other cavalrymen, he already had a bad back.

Because Vincent Charlie's skull had been spared the indignity of being "finished off" with a war club, it was chosen for facial reconstruction by a well-known expert in the field, Betty Pat Gatliff. She took casts and rebuilt the features with clay, using carefully compiled forensic parameters. She used army records and a Victorian-era hair style to represent what Vincent Charlie would have looked like in life. He wasn't a bad-looking guy. Sandy-to-red hair, strong jaw. He probably had bad breath due to poor teeth.

According to witnesses, he was shot "through the hips" as the Lakota and Cheyenne chased a group of soldiers who had ventured too far from Reno's defenses. According to accounts by survivors, he "implored" his fleeing companions not to leave him behind. They promised to return for him, but of course by the time they were able to do that, he was dead. Comparing that bullet-shattered hip bone to the features of the living man is unsettling.

Let me put it this way. As a young man, I was seriously into outdoor sports, including deer hunting. Most deer hunters I know detest what's called an "ass-end" shot—for the animal's suffering, but also the disgust factor, cleaning the carcass. That's with deer. I wince, applying that image to a human being. Young, brown-haired, with hopes, dreams, and fears, Vincent Charlie did not die quickly or easily.

Driving back up from the southern terminus of the National Monument's "Battlefield Road," I came to a pull-out. Getting out to read the interpretive display there, I all but stumbled over Vincent Charlie's headstone, barely off the edge of the asphalt. It was a lonely place to wind up.

Records show that he was from Lucerne, Switzerland, just one more immigrant who came here looking for a better life. Arriving in his new country, I doubt he ever dreamed he'd die at age twenty-eight, up on a God-forsaken hilltop in Montana Territory. The soldiers of empire often wind up just as miserable as the victims of empire.

There were hundreds of Vincent Charlies on that battlefield, and how many millions on the world's battlefields through history? They didn't make the big decisions. Many didn't even want to be there. Yet we called it the "Custer battlefield" to honor the one person who had more choice than anybody? Irony is not always funny.

In 1903, they dug up Vincent Charlie's bones and transferred them to grave #455 in the cemetery. During the four-mile wagon ride, the jostling skeletons of several soldiers got somewhat mixed. His bones shuffled in with those on either side of him, as well as a few mystery bones that never have been identified. Welcome to the world of the enlisted man.

I feel deeply touched by those green recruits, killed before they even learned to shoot an army carbine or ride an army horse. One whole company under Major Reno were such beginners. You can condemn Reno's faults, but he managed to keep most of them alive. That's a sight better than Custer did.

Vincent Charlie was not a new recruit, but he also gets under my skin. Poor, foreign-born lad, crawling after his fleeing comrades with his slow-and-painful-death wound. I put in my military time. I know what it feels like simply to want the "mission" over, whatever it might be, just so I could go home.

Vincent Charlie had no input on army policy toward "Indians" or even 7th Cavalry operations. Then again, I also reflect that the Crow, Lakota, and Cheyenne already *were* home, and received even less consideration than the soldiers. Also, like private soldiers, Crow women like Pretty Shield had relatively meagre input on tribal policy. Ditto Crazy Horse's wife. Ditto a lot of people over the centuries. The ones who make the policies are rarely the ones who bear the cost.

I therefore find it grimly humorous that Custer's bones got lost amid the burials and re-burials after the battle. Cadets and tourists now pay homage to his grave at West Point, but they're most likely worshipping the bones of some unknown, sore-assed buck private. "Once you are dead, . . . all the differences of this world are not important." One can only hope that sustains Libbie Custer, lying in her grave next to a stranger.

If a symbol's meaning lies in what we make of it, I say good for that private. Custer's ego and ambition were mountainous, as were his wife's ambitions for him. For all their charisma, their charity was non-existent. Now fate can smile at their ironic situation. The road is long, but in the end, maybe the arc of the cosmos does bend toward justice.

From another angle, though, Vincent Charlie was also old enough to have taken part in the raid on Black Kettle's camp on the Washita River. What the 7th Cavalry did there—and what they planned to do here on the Little Bighorn—was obscenely hateful. Yet witnessing their remains, I still can't help feeling compassion. It's not, perhaps, as straightforward as the compassion for Manifest Destiny's more obvious victims. But every premature death seems lamentable in its own way.

Artist John Collins' words come into stark relief for me. No matter how different we are, it's not as much as we pretend. The greatest tragedy of the human condition may be that it's so hard to get past those relatively tiny differences until we really are dead. It seems to me that the most challenging courage of "radical hope," is the courage to recognize our commonality with those we consider—or who consider us—less than fully human.

AFTER THAT NOTHING HAPPENED

I admit to feeling a kind of spiritual tension, relaxing after dark in my ultra-light polyester "instant" tent, reading Plenty Coups's remembrances by the glow from my battery-powered LED lantern. I make no excuses. It must be, by Plenty Coups's standards, pretend camping.

Plenty Coups's book ends with a bucolic scene, Linderman, Plenty Coups, and two Crow elders sitting in front of the old chief's square house. Plenty Coups took this occasion to tell of "the wisest man he ever knew," who had the most powerful medicine. He was called, The-Fringe.

As Plenty Coups described him, The-Fringe was a misfit in robust Crow culture. He was gentle, even bashful. He would not bring suffering even to enemies. He did go on the occasional war party, but he never took a scalp, never counted coup, never harmed anyone. The reason his presence on raids was considered valuable was because he was so adept at healing Crow warriors' wounds.

War distinguished a man in Crow life. A man who had never counted coup was not allowed to marry until he reached age twenty-five. In fact, The-Fringe turned thirty, beloved for his wisdom and healing, but still single.

One tribal leader had a daughter called Good Otter. Plenty Coups described The-Fringe's silent love, gazing longingly at this woman from a distance. Sometimes, Plenty Coups said, Good Otter would catch The-Fringe looking at her and smile back. But he never pressed a suit, too bashful to seek a renowned warrior's daughter.

One day Good Otter's eldest brother was badly wounded, fighting the Lakota. He was carried to his father's lodge where The-Fringe heard cries of despair. The-Fringe said nothing, Plenty Coups told Linderman, because by tribal custom a good healer never offers his services. He waits to be asked.

Still, Plenty Coups said, The-Fringe painted himself and prepared his medicine bundle. Sure enough, the wounded warrior's father came and begged for his help. When they returned to his lodge, the wounded man lay beside the fire, tended by the old warrior's wife and Good Otter.

The elder offered "anything I possess" if The-Fringe would save his son. The-Fringe replied with a longing glance across the lodge into the eyes of Good Otter. There was, he said, only one gift he would accept. Even having said that much, though, he hesitated and could go no further.

According to Plenty Coups, Good Otter blurted out, "I am willing." The two elders, listening in, burst out laughing at that point. Plainly, Good Otter knew The-Fringe well enough, she feared he would be too bashful to finish.

Plenty Coups described in detail how The-Fringe worked his healing medicine. The young warrior was saved and The-Fringe and Good Otter married soon after. They were always a loving couple and had children, bringing new life to the village.

I closed the book for a moment and lay there, musing on

how out-of-character this seemed to me. Plenty Coups told many stories of war, hunting, and adventure. But the book ends with what can only be called a romance.

The old chief grew up in a culture that was all about proving one's strength and courage. Even killing an enemy was not the highest grade of honor. It took more courage to strike him with a coup stick or, better yet, one's own hand. To wrest his weapon away from him was yet better, or to lead a successful war party, or to steal enemy horses.

Plenty Coups did all these things. The-Fringe did none. It seems to me, Plenty Coups's final story embodied the way the Crow's world had turned on end. Old rules, even the old standard of what made a man a man, no longer applied. That's what it meant to "walk in the dark," as both Plenty Coups and Pretty Shield described it, through a world they no longer understood. War was no longer the highest achievement. They had to find new "folkways," as Jonathan Lear terms it, strategies to take them forward in an increasingly unknown world. As—frankly—Euro-Americans may find themselves required to do soon enough.

Lear doesn't mention The-Fringe in *Radical Hope*. But The-Fringe's story does not merely capsulize Lear's analysis of the drastic changes in the Crow's world. It also tells me that Plenty Coups saw the same changes Lear saw, long before Lear was even born.

What Lear calls "existing folkways," the means by which Plenty Coups led his people into their uncertain future, are broad and subtle. Though the old chief claimed "nothing happened" after moving onto the reservation, he actually remained active for another forty years, lobbying for Crow interests in Washington, D.C. and Montana's State Capitol. There's nothing surprising to me about a successful leader from any culture schmoozing and negotiating as part of their political tool kit. That is, however, why Crazy Horse was rejected as a leader by his people. He eschewed the strategies Plenty Coups so ably pursued. And while Sitting Bull understood leadership, he likewise failed because he could not see what the Crow elders saw, that drastically changing times demanded change and subtlety in tactics, as well.

Because Linderman was a well-known Montana journalist and politician, I think Plenty Coups' conversations with him were one more piece of the canny old chief's strategy. Plenty Coups knew Linderman could sway white opinion, and implored him to "Do all you can." Plenty Coups reminded him both of the Crow's suffering and the Crow's service to white people, then ended by saying, "I am done. The story telling is finished."

Linderman entreated Plenty Coups to tell more, but the old chief poignantly refused. "When the buffalo went away, the hearts of my people fell to the ground and they could not lift them up again. After that, nothing happened." I can picture the look on the old man's face as he said, "You know that part of my life as well as I do. You saw what happened to us when the buffalo went away." That was the exchange which inspired Lear's book on the Crow's "cultural devastation."

To Lear, Plenty Coups embodies "a form of courage that Sitting Bull [and Crazy Horse] did not grasp." That is, the Crow's resistance took a more subtle, resilient form. They saw the futility of open war, and accepted inevitable change, while fighting for the limited victories attainable to them. They retained their identity, kept the traditions which fed them and worked for them, kept what they could, sacrificed what they had to. More than a century before the term survivance was applied to the indigenous struggle, they were practicing it. Even in the face of, as Lear put it, a future so changed, they could not foresee it in detail until it was upon them.

RADICAL HOPE AND SURVIVANCE

$\mathcal{D}$riving away from Little Bighorn Battlefield, I found myself on a corduroy-rough dirt road west of Hardin, Montana. Chief Plenty Coups's homestead was my next stop. There was no campground there, so I would have to reach it before day's end. Plenty Coups State Park would, my guidebook said, close at five o'clock, so I needed to hurry.

My dirt road shortcut actually slowed me down. I came to a ribbon of two-lane blacktop with no road signs and no iPhone reception. Welcome to the "Res." Comparing paper maps, I estimated this was the road I wanted. I turned and rolled down what seemed an endless series of valleys while the afternoon ticked away.

Schedules can be terrible things. Looking back, I let mine distract me from the austere grandeur unfolding around me. Plenty Coups thought this land the most beautiful in the world. Sprawling vistas crept by, looming bluffs, expanses of prairie dry and challenging except for a reedy stream now and then, meandering casually along a valley floor.

After a few hours of white man's hurry, I did arrive at a

patch of buildings marked Pryor, Montana. With relief, I certified my navigation as adequate. Signage guided me the rest of the way to Chief Plenty Coups State Park. I pulled into the parking lot and forced myself to settle back into be-in-this-place mind. It was another refined nugget of the tension between my way of life and Plenty Coups's. I'd burned a lot of petrol and nervous energy, I reflected. A key part of my culture's difference from his might just consist of that: tight schedules and nervous energy.

The visitors center stood low and circular, designed, I think, to evoke the shape of a tipi. Low, round roof, walls the color of the prairie grass. I decided to save it for last so I could take more time exploring the grounds.

In the space of only a few years, in the late 1880s, the Crow were forcibly transformed from nomads following the buffalo, to sedentary life on the reservation. Secure in Euro-American resolve to teach "Indians" a "better" way of life, the US government told them they had to give up their tipis and build log cabins, which the Crow called, "square houses."

Tipis were light and airy, easily built and moved, cool in summer, snug in winter. None of that applied to "square house" log cabins. Such forced changes altered everything the Crow knew about living and about themselves. Having pushed hard for accommodation and adaptation, Plenty Coups resolutely threw himself into cabin building and farming. He made himself the example.

In 1883, he built a large cabin along with an outbuilding to use as a trading post. Later, as he and his wife neared death in the 1930s, he willed his property to the state of Montana as a park. He desired, he said, to share his land with all people. I also wonder if he had ulterior motives. Perhaps the more white people knew about the Crow, the more even-handed might be their dealings.

Treetops two hundred yards away marked where Pryor

Creek wound, as I followed a twenty-first-century sidewalk from the visitors center to a grove of towering cottonwoods and a large log house. In front of it, to my surprise, stood a tipi. As it turns out, even though Plenty Coups conscientiously led the movement to adapt to white people's ways and live in Euro-American-style houses, he was unable to sleep in one himself. He went back to sleeping outside in his tipi.

I poked my head in through the flap and natural aromas filled my nostrils. A tipi is about as organic as you can get: lodge poles, rawhide ropes, and buffalo-hide cover, tanned and stitched. Everything in it was derived from hoof, claw, wing, or root. I couldn't help wondering again, if only for an instant, what Plenty Coups would think of the tent in which I slept: ultra-light metals and refined petroleum products.

The tipi was roomier inside than I expected. I read that a lining can be hung inside to insulate and direct air flow in cold weather. Smoke from a central fire is guided up and out a smoke hole at the apex. Tent flaps around the smoke hole, called "ears," can be adjusted to regulate the draft. Then in summer, the lining is removed and the tipi's lower hem can be folded up to let cool night air circulate. A half dozen people could sleep comfortably. A big tipi could hold a council circle of two dozen or more.

The tipi was, I read, the woman's realm. Women sewed the buffalo-hide covering, assembled the lodges, and took them down when it was time to move. What went on inside was at the sufferance of the woman. Plenty Coups's house may have been built and rebuilt according to his plan. But when he entered his tipi in the evening, he was stepping into the domain of his wife, Strikes-the-Iron. There, he would follow her rules.

It was not lost on me that Plenty Coups told Linderman little about his private life. Or that perhaps Linderman had simply not transcribed that part of their conversations. Either way, I was doubly appreciative that Linderman had interviewed Pretty Shield, and that I enjoyed the benefit of that broadened view.

I walked on to the house. It was built out of square, unfinished timbers, chinked with clay. The structure had long since weathered gray. According to the brochure, during one of Plenty Coups' trips to Washington, D.C., he was inspired by a visit to George Washington's estate, Mount Vernon. Eyeing the main section of his cabin, I saw dormer windows on the top story that did, to me, echo Mount Vernon.

My steps sounded across the porch and across the softwood floor. It was frontier architecture, similar to the oldest buildings at Fort Robinson. Including the guardhouse where Crazy Horse was killed. That returned me to reflecting on the differing Crow and Lakota struggles in the face of Euro-American expansion. Sitting Bull and Crazy Horse fought like wildcats, were both martyred—"went down fighting" as Jonathan Lear would put it—and are famous icons of indigenous resistance. I had never even heard of Plenty Coups or Pretty Shield before I set out on this journey. Plenty Coups's resistance was too subtle to register on Euro-Americans as real resistance. This might be, I suspect, one reason it was more effective. The Crow lost much, but managed to retain more than most other First Nations, including the Lakota. I find that worth remembering as we balance between fierceness and subtlety in resisting oppressive systems. That's not to condemn fierceness, but very much to express admiration for subtlety.

To me, Plenty Coups's relative success puts a human face on the difference between resistance and survivance. Crazy Horse and Sitting Bull resisted unto death, "went down fighting," took a fair number of whites with them, and became the stuff of legend. They left glorious legacies, but their heroism did not save their people. I had, for days, been witnessing how such glory leads mainly to graves on hillsides.

Plenty Coups went for the limited-but-achievable victory. He resigned himself to white perversity and out-and-out perfidy, but engaged and learned Euro-American ways. The difference in results between the two responses is not black-and-white, but it is real. Crow children did not have to suffer through hellish white mission schools the way children of other Nations did. The Crow's Reservation never got sectioned off, parts of it grabbed by white entrepreneurs, the way Lakota and Ute land did, and that of other Nations. There is poverty on the Crow's Reservation as well as others, but not as much.

On the other hand, had the Lakota and Cheyenne not fought Euro-American expansion, would there have been reason for the army to seek Crow and Shoshone allies in the first place? The Crow leaders' more subtle road was part of a larger system. We can see how the pieces fit together one hundred years later. It had to be much more difficult to sort out such things when one was standing right in the midst of them.

Still, Lear's assessment of Plenty Coups gives us hints to go by. In the end, I think, it would be a blunder to consider Plenty Coups's survivance strategy a whit less courageous than heroic resistance. The real art would lie in finding the fine line between the extremes: futile heroics on the one side, despair or magical thinking on the other.

One could call Wovoka's Ghost Dancing prophesy one example of magical thinking. He claimed that pure religious practice, with no further mechanism, would make the white hoards vanish and the wild game return. It's ironic that Euro-American cultural paranoia made the Ghost Dance seem threatening enough to kill three hundred unarmed villagers.

But that also suggests retreat into self-delusion is hardly confined to one culture. The difference would be that the dominant culture, being dominant, can luxuriate in its conceits.

SQUARE HOUSE AND MEDICINE SPRING

I walked on into Plenty Coups's square house. An imposing bust of the old chief dominated the lower floor, gazing implacably from a shoulder-high wooden pedestal. People had left offerings before it: folded bills, cigarettes, coins, even cans of beer and food items.

Studying the iconic old leader, I mused that Pretty Shield sometimes disagreed with Plenty Coups, and didn't hesitate to mention mistakes he had made. To her, he was still just a human being. Would she have left offerings? I wondered. I doubted it. But I also doubted she would have stood in her grandchildren's way if they had wanted to.

Traveling to Washington, D.C., Plenty Coups skillfully and persistently lobbied Congress. Such strategy kept the Crow Reservation mostly intact and its resources in Crow hands. Sitting Bull considered Plenty Coups a coward, but the old chief's results speak for themselves.

To me, Lear's definition of radical hope seems a bit fuzzy. He calls it a commitment "to a future goodness that transcends the current ability to understand what it is." How could it be other than fuzzy when there's no schematic for working through such changed times? The trick would be to know which traditions to keep and which to relinquish. After all, Lakota and Cheyenne (and Crow) warrior practice would also be a folkway, to use Lear's term.

I don't think it's coincidence that Gerald Vizenor's definition of survivance is just as fuzzy. "Survivance," he writes, "is an active sense of presence, the continuance of Native stories, not a mere reaction . . . . Native survivance stories are renunciations of dominance, tragedy, and victimry." He goes on to say that his definition is deliberately imprecise, an inspiration to creativity.

Add in survivance as I first heard it defined, "survival plus resistance," and the mud does begin to settle. Survival and resistance together, fueled alike by hope and commitment to the *achievable* "future goodness."

Again, I've seen no sign that Lear ever read Vizenor. The commonality between them comes from within the ideas themselves. It also strikes me that the Crow elders' nuance and subtlety also involved a sense of human commonality. The-Fringe's story certainly hints toward the worth of human universals: life, love, compassion, as opposed to differences between groups' identities.

This leads me back to the most non-warrior medicine creature imaginable, the chickadee, which the Crow took as their guide to the future. The chickadee only *appears* to be tiny and helpless. In Crow lore, it thrives by listening and learning from the mistakes of others, that is, the mistakes of one's enemies. More commonality, subtle but identifiable. Plenty Coups's diplomatic skills keyed on common ethos and common interest. And a look to the long game.

Thus reflecting, I explored the house upstairs and down. As I came back downstairs past a window, I noticed a black swallowtail butterfly, beating its wings against one pane. Insect fashion, it saw only one path, straight through the impermeable glass. Knowing that it would struggle against that window until it died, I cupped it between my hands, carried it outside, and let it go. It fluttered toward some willows downhill from me and faded from view.

I followed it, making my way down the walkway to Plenty Coups's medicine spring. A large signboard warned me, due to fertilizer and pesticide runoff from local agriculture, the spring's water could not be certified safe to drink. Even at that, I later learned, some Crow still use the water for ritual and to cure sickness. One online account I read told how a sickly baby was given a few drops of the medicine water and regained her robustness through its curative properties. The symbolism was worth it, apparently.

The spring was nothing special to look at, just a dark pool set about by willows and some cottonwoods. Leaves and dust floated on the surface. I smelled moist earth and thick foliage all around me. I crossed a little wooden bridge where a stream flowed out, then followed the path around to a shady area. More offerings had been laid beside the water. Ribbons and dollar bills had been knotted around overhanging willow branches. I wondered how people chose what part of themselves to leave behind.

A Zen monk could sit here, I reflected, and feel right at home. There's a kind of power to acceptance and patience, which opens doors in the mind. One settles into one's own core. A person could do that here. I could envy Plenty Coups the time he spent gazing into the water, singing to himself. But his reflective time, unlike Crazy Horse's, was fuel for larger work, face-to-face wheedling and negotiating with white powers that be, whom Crazy Horse would have curtly dismissed as kill-or-be-killed "enemy."

COMMONALITY

fter a while, I wandered back up to the visitors center. As I walked across the parking lot, I saw a worn minivan with South Dakota license plates pull in. A tall, heavy-set man with long, black hair got out the driver's side. From the other emerged his plump wife, who retrieved two small children from the back.

From their features, flowing hair, and the traditionally styled beadwork on their jeans, they were unmistakably "Indian and proud of it," as their bumper sticker read. Leading one child by the hand, pushing the other in a stroller, they walked ahead of me into the building.

They seemed to enjoy themselves as they studied the exhibits of Crow culture and art. The Crow are noted for beadwork and horsemanship. The couple smiled, pointed, and explained something to their older child in a language I didn't understand. They closely examined a large display of the chickadee and its meaning in Crow life.

I couldn't resist eavesdropping as they stopped to chat in English with the state park person at the counter. It turned out they were, of all possible coincidences, Lakota. They had driven here from South Dakota's Cheyenne River Reservation, they said, because they liked to visit other First Nation cultural sites.

Now this is something, I thought to myself. I hadn't stopped to think that in our day, one indigenous culture would want to learn about another. Especially given the similarities, also historic enmity, between Crow and Lakota.

But that says more about my own naïveté than it says about indigenous culture. Survivance is communal practice. The Lakota were the strongest of the Great Plains Nations until the 1860s, and as far as at least some other Nations were concerned, they had the arrogance that comes with power. But they've had a century and a half to suffer and reflect. Their survivance is the hard-learned product of experience even more severe than that of the Crow.

Marty Two Bulls, Sr. writes on Lakota experience, "[We] are citizens of two countries, and have learned to survive in both." They know what they lost and how it was lost. How simple to unite with former enemies in common cause?

It also strikes me Euro-American culture is where the Lakota were, relatively speaking, when Lewis and Clark encountered them in 1803. The explorers described them as "powerful and arrogant," similar to descriptions I've heard applied to the United States in our time. It would be, I think, self-indulgent to apply such a term as "survivance" to Euro-Americans, dominant culture that we are. And what superhuman wisdom would it take, in our privilege, to appreciate wisdom that comes from real suffering.

But I predict that will someday change. Then the question will be, how long will it take Euro-Americans to learn the craft our indigenous neighbors have been studying for more than a century?

It's no wonder winter would find me watching First Nations gather at the Standing Rock Reservation, opposing the Dakota Access Pipeline. White allies treated the Dakota Access standoff as a kind of environmental be-all and end-all. To indigenous peoples, though, it was just one more confrontation in a very long process.

They survive despite facing multi-level cultural insensitivity and greed. They survive and remember who they are. I observe that Euro-Americans are given to a level of "victory or defeat" thinking, forcing a conclusion in a limited time frame, where disadvantaged cultures understand the ongoing nature of survival and resistance. As Jonathan Lear might observe, Euro-Americans don't yet recognize that future so changed we don't yet know what it is. We don't recognize it, but that doesn't mean it's not out there.

At any rate, at Chief Plenty Coups State Park, I watched one discrete example of First Nations maintaining lives and identities by plunging into their own rich diversity. I observed from a distance that techniques of survivance may succeed most where they are least recognized by the powers that be.

SITTING BULL

By 1886, the Crow's world had turned upside down. They had moved onto the Reservation, the buffalo were all but gone. In September of that year, the Lakota war chief, Sitting Bull, paid them a visit. According to historian Frederick E. Hoxie, Sitting Bull went with Crow leaders to view the Little Bighorn Battlefield. "Look at that monument," Hoxie quotes him, gesturing toward Last Stand Hill. "That marks the work of *our* people." He condemned Plenty Coups's judgment and courage. As far as Sitting Bull was concerned, no strong leader would co-operate with the American government.

Pretty Shield tells a different story. According to her, Sitting Bull visited Crow Agency with one hundred followers for four days of feasting and dancing. She doesn't mention the visit to the battlefield. Instead, she describes a conclave the final day. Sitting Bull walked to the middle of the council circle and sat with a fancy rifle across his lap. He wore beautiful clothes, she said, and "to me, he looked proud."

A Crow chief named Crazy Head walked out and confronted Sitting Bull. "How can a man who thinks himself great be unkind to his own people?" Crazy Head demanded. Crazy Head then described the coups he had counted on Lakota warriors in past battles, then wheeled, snatched Sitting Bull's rifle, and threw it into the crowd. Finally, Crazy Head pushed Sitting Bull over on his back and leaped over him.

That strikes me as a mortal insult. But as Pretty Shield tells it, Sitting Bull's followers only laughed at him. "Sitting Bull was unkind," she said, then added that his own people feared him, but did not love him.

Commenting on Pretty Shield's account, Linderman proposed that Crazy Head's act was just a way of re-counting coup. Still, it seems to me, it cannot be taken as other than an insult. So did this insult come after—or possibly because—Sitting Bull insulted Plenty Coups? All I know is that within four years, Sitting Bull was dead, shot in the head by one of his own people.

Jonathan Lear visits Hoxie's version in *Radical Hope*, and contrasts Sitting Bull's resolve to go down fighting versus Plenty Coup's more subtle, persistent courage. If, as Lear defines it, radical hope is "commitment to a future goodness that transcends the current ability to understand what it is," Sitting Bull was clinging to the past he knew, while Plenty Coups led his people into a misty future.

I see a risk of sentimentality in either strategy. Sitting Bull and Crazy Horse's warrior legacy is famous, the stuff of many a Hollywood motion picture. It's also possible to sentimentalize the Crow people, though, giving up the warrior life, becoming chickadees, learning from the mistakes of others. Crow and Lakota folkways are almost identical. One could say Sitting Bull and the Crow elders merely chose different arrows from quivers that were about the same. Pretty Shield makes clear, the Crow were awash in doubt and dismay at the time.

SWORD BEARER'S REVOLT

*L*ear examines another account from Hoxie as well, a tragedy Plenty Coups didn't mention to Linderman. Perhaps it was one of the memories Plenty Coups meant when he said, "You saw what happened when the buffalo went away." His silence hints how distressing were the moral and ethical adjustments he had to make.

As Hoxie drew the scene, Crow, Lakota, and Cheyenne were resigned to reservation life, the old ways behind them. They began to speak to one another in new ways, Sitting Bull's visit to Crow Agency being part of a nationwide trend. To some Crow, though, Sitting Bull embodied nostalgia for the old life. Meanwhile, below the cordial surface, enmity still lingered. As Hoxie's and Pretty Shield's accounts both show.

Crow youth must sort out their place in this confusing picture. In spring, 1887, several Crow youth attend a sun dance on Montana's Cheyenne reservation. One youth dances magnificently. He also has a medicine dream which impresses his hosts. They present him with a ceremonial sword and a new name, Sword Bearer.

Sword Bearer is young, passionate, and idealistic. His hosts tell him the sword's medicine will protect him from the white man's bullets. The Ghost Dancers likewise believe their shirts will protect them from bullets.

A month later some Blackfeet men raid a Crow village and steal horses, another lingering piece of the old ways. Sword Bearer leads several young Crow in a reprisal raid. They take the horses back, killing some Blackfeet in the process. By tradition, this is a noble victory.

Their celebration takes them to Crow Agency. The whites may have tamed the old men, Sword Bearer believes, but he and his friends are untamed young warriors. They show this by riding through Crow Agency, shouting and shooting into the air. When the angry agent comes out to upbraid them, Sword Bearer leaps off his horse, runs up the front steps, and pushes the agent back with the barrel of his rifle. From Sword Bearer's point of view, the gesture is a high-spirited coup. That never occurs to the Euro-American agent, who interprets it as a lethal threat.

Shaken, the agent flees inside, locks the door, and telegraphs Fort Custer about the "death threat." Word of the confrontation spreads, and the Billings newspaper publishes an editorial about the "Indian uprising." The Crow need to be lashed back into line, the paper says.

Tensions skyrocket. Sword Bearer insists that Crow leaders must fight. After all, that's what Sitting Bull and Crazy Horse would do. The Crow chiefs, sadder and wiser, see Sword Bearer as a charismatic, but dangerous hothead. He might have been a rising leader a decade earlier, but his actions now threaten the Crow with a war the elders do not want and know they cannot win.

Things come to a head when a hundred Crow warriors find themselves in a stare-down against a company of soldiers with Hotchkiss guns. Sword Bearer is there with his sword. A few shots are exchanged, but Plenty Coups, Crazy Head, and the other elders intercede to prevent worse violence. Over Sword Bearer's protest, the elders persuade most young Crow men to lay down their weapons and surrender.

Seeing things go against him, Sword Bearer tries to flee, only to be shot and killed by a tribal policeman. Ironically, this is the same way Sitting Bull died. Seven other rebels wind up in the agency stockade, faced with prison for rebellion.

Reflecting on this, I see Sword Bearer exuding the same level of courage Plenty Coups possessed as a young man. But he didn't have Plenty Coups's subtlety and political awareness. Lear presents him as the embodiment of "go down fighting" resistance, as opposed to the radical hope and survivance of the Crow elders.

To me, this also points up a heartbreaking aspect of survivance. Forced to choose between old ways and current necessity, Plenty Coups and the elders suffered the rebels' arrest and Sword Bearer's death. They were playing a long game beyond Sword Bearer's ken. But it had to be a heart-wrenching choice.

I came across an old photograph of Plenty Coups visiting the prisoners at the stockade. They're posed on the building's porch with watchful army guards standing behind them. Plenty Coups stands to one side, looking forlorn. How could he not? Moving into an uncertain future, the most bitter pill of all had to be siding with white soldiers against Crow youth who displayed the very virtues that made Plenty Coups himself a leader a generation earlier.

The Crow elders played a bad hand as best they could, negotiating grazing rights, mineral rights, and a railroad right-of-way against an endless series of inroads. It took patient and persistent greatness to come away with anything. But the sacrifice of traditional autonomy and traditional ways had to be most difficult.

How surprising can it be that Plenty Coups would not tell Linderman such stories? From the look on his face in that old photograph, taken after negotiating the arrest of the ringleaders, Plenty Coups must have felt like a knife that had stabbed his Nation's finest young men in the back. Neither he nor Pretty Shield mentioned the so-called Crow Revolt to Linderman. What could they have said without weeping?

Plenty Coups never mentioned Sitting Bull's visit, either. He only said, "Listening as the chickadee listens, we saw that those who made war against the white man only failed in the end and lost their land. Now they hate the ground that holds their lodges."

He told Linderman that he fought alongside the whites "not because I love the white man, but because I saw that this was the only way we could keep our lands." "The Cheyenne and the Sioux," he mused, "have always been our enemies. But I am sorry for them today."

Reflecting on this, I once more conclude that I need to use the term survivance with humility. I cannot claim it as my own, only as a source of learning. My forbears may have been dirt-poor farmers, but at least they could choose the dirt they farmed. They could travel to a strange town without being stared at. They could keep the faith and life assumptions they brought from Europe.

I don't have to be rich or have lots of employees to be a fourth-generation colonizer. It's my core reality. I can feel grief of survivance, but only when I pause to think about it. It does not come of my own or my forbears' experience.

A LIFE WE DO NOT KNOW

*S*hortly before Plenty Coups died at age eighty-four, Frank Linderman brought him a freshly published copy of the book, which came out of their interviews. A photograph shows the great chief, deep in wrinkles and white hair, posing with the finished volume. Plenty Coups was almost blind by that time. In the photo, he looks not at the book he holds, but stares off into space. One wonders, is he seeing some past glory? Travels to Washington, D.C. to lobby for the few rights and the little land that remained to his people? Or is he thinking of Sword Bearer?

Experts in various fields predict the future, and are, often as not, laughably wide of the mark. Looking forward from 1887 to the world the Crow would inhabit at the end of his years, "a world he did not know," Plenty Coups could hardly have expected to do better. He did, however, assay with impressive accuracy the *approach* that would best take his people through those mists. "Radical hope . . . is directed toward a future goodness that transcends the current ability to understand what it is." Lear's words are not to be underestimated, either for their subtlety or their degree of difficulty.

Plenty Coups's late-life activities are documented in word, picture, and even the Congressional Record. Then again, for Plenty Coups to describe his legal and congressional advocacy, he really would need terminology Linderman probably knew better than he did.

In his most famous statement to his people, Plenty Coups said, "Education is your greatest weapon. With education, you are the white man's equal, without education you are his victim." Nor did he settle for the brutal missionary schools foisted on too many indigenous children. He insisted the tribal school be moved from Crow Agency to Pryor, where he and Crow parents could keep an eye on it. I believe that in his last years, the canny old Chief cultivated his relationship with Linderman precisely as one more card to play for the future of his people.

Strategic use of "white man's education" might have been intuitive, but other strategies were so counter-intuitive as to seem inexplicable, at least on the surface.

With Plenty Coups's urging and support, young Crow men volunteered to fight beside white soldiers in the First World War. Crow men would serve with distinction in the Second World War, as well. One, Joseph Medicine Crow, became a legitimate war hero, then went on to become the first Crow to earn a Ph.D.

Of his military service, Joseph Medicine Crow stated that young Crow men went to war for the United States "to give back" as Americans. I did a double take when I read that. What did they owe our government? It seems to me they were responding to a deeper commonality. Deeper community. I think Euro-Americans such as myself need to take a hard look at that. If there is an abiding spirit we can all share, it has to come out of that level of sophistication and generosity.

Plenty Coups adopted Roman Catholicism in 1917,

though he also continued to practice his tribal religion. He managed his trading post and his log "square house." He slept in his tipi outside. He rode in white people's parades.

When the First World War ended, he was the only indigenous leader invited to dedicate the Tomb of the Unknown Soldier. He laid a war bonnet and coup stick on top of the tomb, and said that he hoped there would be no further wars. As we know too well, the changing world has never changed *that* much! I would be surprised if Plenty Coups, fitting though his words were for the occasion, didn't fully understand that in the long run, human nature would inter that peace ceremony with all the other white people's promises.

He was wise enough to know what a victory of survivance looks like. In 1908, for example, Montana's congressional delegation made an all-out effort to open the Crow Reservation to white settlers, same as the Dawes Allotment Act had opened other First Nations lands twenty years earlier. The Crow united behind Plenty Coups's lobbying efforts against the legislation. Plenty Coups testified before congressional hearings, aided by the first generation of young Crow lawyers to pass through the white-style educational system. Finally, at a Senate hearing in 1917, the bill's sponsor, Montana Senator Thomas Walsh, withdrew his legislation.

After the hearing, a jocular Plenty Coups approached Walsh and tapped the Senator lightly on the shoulder with his cane. The Senator may have considered it a strange joke or even a friendly gesture. But the Crow delegation with Plenty Coups had to know exactly what that meant.

That had to be one of those special moments when the old language held, even if within a totally different context. After all, Vizenor's definition of survivance did urge First Nations to express their lives in their own terms. Plenty Coups lived the full definition before it was ever written. It embodied immense spiritual sophistication, defining "spiritual" the way I, as an atheist, can define it.

Still, in every source I perused, the pain comes through. In old age, Plenty Coups and Pretty Shield would both say the lives they led had become "unnatural." In his last years, Plenty Coups was anxious, as he put it, to go to his father, the Creator, and live again as people were meant to live.

Pretty Shield expressed sadness in her own way. "The happiest days of my life were spent following the buffalo over our beautiful country," she told Linderman. "I believed everything was good on this world."

She explained how her heart "fell down when I began to see dead buffalo scattered all over our beautiful country." She recounted the herds of buffalo shot, the skins stripped off, the bodies left to rot by white hide hunters. The land lay heavy with the stench so bad, she said, a person couldn't even smell the spring flowers. "The white man did this, even when he did not want the meat."

She told Linderman about white cowboys who encountered a Crow boy with a disability: he could neither hear nor speak. Because he couldn't answer their questions, they put a rope around him and dragged him to death. She told about her daughters dying of white people's diseases. So that in her old age, Pretty Shield had to bring up her grandchildren in a world she herself did not understand.

But you know, she said, "I do not hate *anybody*, not even the white man." She must have emphasized "anybody," because Linderman puts it in italics. "I knew that this would only make things worse for me. But he changed everything for us, did many bad deeds before we got used to him."

My father's ancestors came to this continent, at least in part, as a product of mid-nineteenth century European tumult in general and the Irish potato famine in particular. The Great Hunger, I've heard it called, and described as genocide committed by Ireland's British occupiers. Now my loved ones and I live on land from which North America's indigenous peoples were driven by a genocide that worked better for us.

Nothing is more amazing to me than the sweeping tides of human development. I yearn toward nurse log benevolence, myself being spawned by millennia of human overthrow and despair. Any good or loving act I accomplish has its deepest roots in such tides of suffering, in ground fertilized by genocide, blood of my blood, bone of my bone. That doesn't make my love any less. It makes my humility profound. And my confusion continual.

When one is of the dominant culture, confusion might not be a bad practice from time to time. Humility is, after all, a difficult discipline. I don't do it as often or as well as I would like. Same with compassion, patience—wisdom. As a middle class Euro-American, I do not need to practice survivance. I can only study it as a greater wisdom, something to which I can aspire in preparation for "cultural devastation" on a drastically different scale.

I wish Pretty Shield could have been in that hearing room when Plenty Coups tapped Senator Walsh on the shoulder with his cane. If radical hope and survivance lie in using existing folkways to seek "a future goodness that transcends the current ability to understand what it is," I also find myself pondering what that term, "existing folkways," might mean in Euro-American culture. Lear uses the Crow's history as education. Euro-Americans would do well to seek commonality with that spirit.

PART VI
LIVING ON THE CALDERA

We live [with] a heightened sense that civilizations are themselves vulnerable . . . , an uncanny sense of menace . . . . Perhaps if we could give a name to our shared sense of vulnerability, we could find better ways to live with it.

—Jonathan Lear, *Radical Hope: Ethics in the Face of Cultural Devastation*

ROCK CREEK CAMPGROUND

*A*ugust 17, 1959, a seventy-nine-year-old woman named
*Grace Miller finishes her day at the tourist lodge she
operates on Montana's Hebgen Lake. She closes up shop, walks a
few yards to her own house, and goes to bed for the night.*

*Jolted awake in her bed, she senses that something is drastically
wrong. She stares into the darkness, trying to understand. She
hears a freight-train rumbling past her bedroom window. Then she
remembers—there are no railroad tracks in this valley!*

*She scrambles out of bed and down the stairs. Her malamute
dog runs after her, its nails scrabbling on the wood floor that trem-
bles beneath them. When she tries to push her front door open, it's
jammed. Clenching her teeth, she throws herself against it, it flies
open, and she lurches out onto her front porch.*

*The roaring is all around her. She feels as though she's on an
elevator going downward, and sees the earth before her sliding up
and away in the moonlight, opening a chasm. Her house is sliding
into Hebgen Lake!*

*With a cry, she leaps for her life. She lands on the other side of
the fissure, knocking the breath out of her. Her malamute lands
next to her as she rolls over and tries to sit up. The whole hill is*

shaking, bouncing her butt on the gravelly ground as her house parades down into the water. At last, just the peak of the roof pokes up.

Realizing she has just lived through an earthquake that probably should have killed her, she begins to tremble. Her house and the lodge next door have both settled out into the lake. She's now thirty feet above them, so far up from the water, the big waves kicked up by the earthquake don't even make her wet. In the shock of the moment, she's not as surprised that her house is gone as that the roof is off level.

Miles up Highway 287, beyond Hebgen Lake's dam, August 17 marks the height of the summer camping season. Nestled between high canyon walls, scenic Rock Creek Campground filled early in the day. Later arrivals had to take "overflow" places downstream or farther up the mountainside.

Aromas of pine, smoke from campfires, sounds of camping all drift in the evening air. Laughter echoes from playing children. Ever present is the rushing sound of the Madison River a few yards downhill. The evening fades, so do the voices and aromas. People zip up tent flaps and crawl into sleeping bags. By 11:30, only a couple campfires still burn.

At 11:37, the world roars and shakes like a grizzly bear tearing into a food locker. Trees sway and crack, picnic tables bounce like toys, boulders jounce down the mountainside, crashing off trees and into parked cars.

The mountain above them thunders like all the devils in hell being disemboweled at once. The whole mountainside crushes downward, millions of tons of rocks, trees, and earth. It's the last sound nineteen of Rock Creek Campground's campers ever hear as the landslide buries them beneath three hundred feet of debris. In the following days, rescue workers will not even try to recover the bodies.

Up at the overflow campsites, boulders crash past and trees topple. After the thunder comes the roar of water, washed over

Hebgen Lake's dam, slashing down the canyon. It washes away tents and cars. Once the chaos goes quiet, survivors feel about for loved ones in the darkness. They fumble for lanterns and flash-lights, and try to find cars that might still run. Groans from the injured, sobs, shouts of misery and fear fill the night. Morning will be a long time coming.

In southwest Montana the lower Madison River has carved a canyon deep into layers of metamorphic schist and gneiss. Against that harder stone, a quarter-mile-thick layer of pink dolomite once loomed over Rock Creek Campground like the Sword of Damocles. Those layers were all laid down flat millions of years before the dinosaurs roamed. It took a westward-drifting continent and eons of stone bending and buckling to turn the flat layers into ridges.

August 17, 1959, continental plates twenty miles down slipped past one another a good thirty feet. This released energy equal to hundred of nuclear warheads, and produced an earthquake that changed the landscape from western Wyoming to the Continental Divide. It brought millions of tons of dolomite crashing to the canyon floor. I was a kid in Grand Junction, Colorado, four hundred miles away. Even there, it was big news.

I didn't dream of geological scale back then. But a friend's family was camping at nearby Yellowstone Park when the quake hit. They brought back nightmare stories of swaying trees, bouncing cars, and pavement buckling like clay in the hands of an angry God. I didn't know whether to be impressed or jealous. I think I was both.

Now, five decades later, I was finally visiting the earth-quake zone. A day after the thoughtful shade of Chief Plenty Coups State Park, I drove toward the Continental Divide. I'm a wandering Colorado native. These mountains felt like loving arms, welcoming me home. Then again, the 1959 earthquake showed how violent these mountains could be.

EARTHQUAKE LAKE

*H*ebgen Lake lay broad and serene to my left, mile after mile beneath autumn's sun. Fishing resorts still dotted the shoreline. Almost sixty years old, the earthquake's slide face loomed, raw and bare as though new, on my other side. Over the decades, the state of Montana had installed miles of roadside interpretive displays, to document the catastrophe. I stopped to read each marker.

Following signage, I turned down a short gravel track to found myself on an older strip of asphalt, which paralleled the highway. I stopped, got out, and read yet another display. It informed me that this was a strip of old Highway 287, chopped off by the earthquake and abandoned. Yellow tassels of grass poked up through cracks in the asphalt, bowing in the morning breeze. The old road signs still stood here and there, faded yellow. Flecks of yellow paint still marked what had been the center line. I walked to the pavement's broken end and looked straight down at water, twenty feet below. A quarter mile away, on the far side of a stark cliff, I could see the pavement start up again.

I read yet another display, which told the story of Grace

Miller's lodge, her slide down to the lake, and her leap for life out her own front door. Hebgen Lake has twenty-one square miles of surface area, it said, but the earthquake sloshed that water like a small wash basin. It created a freshwater tsunami, called a *seiche,* which overtopped the dam by eight feet.

I walked back to my car, pulled back up to the new highway, and drove on. New trees had sprung up along the rift, some of them now forty feet high. I passed Hebgen Lake Dam, high and commanding, solid enough to survive while the earthquake toppled a whole mountainside. Then I came to a second lake, long and narrow between steep canyon walls. This was Earthquake Lake, formed when that mountainside collapsed and blocked the river farther downstream.

Dead conifers poked up from this lake, skeletons of forest that drowned as the water rose. They went on for miles. Ahead, the highway wound uphill and onto an immense barricade of pink stone. That was the collapsed dolomite ridge which had buried Rock Creek Campground. A modernistic visitor center stood atop that mammoth sill. High up the mountainside, across the river from me, I could see the cyclopean scar which marked where dolomite ridge had once loomed.

I parked downhill from the visitors center, got out, and yet another marker told me I was standing atop rubble one hundred yards deep. Somewhere, three hundred feet below my shoes, lay the skeletons of those nineteen campers. All about me stood huge, pink boulders, as though dumped there yesterday by the hands of the gods. I walked to the edge and peered down. The Madison River rushed through a cut far below me, and on down to a green valley beyond.

The mass seemed unimaginable. Blocks of stone the size of apartment houses rested on the mountainside far above me, dwarfing the tourists climbing past them. That they moved at all was overawing. That they rolled that far, that fast—down the mountain, clear across the canyon, then well up the far slope—there are no words.

Those poor campers. The very existence of Rock Creek Campground shows that in 1959, no one foresaw how this picturesque canyon was a trap waiting to spring. That dolomite waited millions of years to collapse; just a matter of time until the earth's ever-creeping crust would shake hard enough. Yet earthquakes happen all the time. The ridge's collapse was, then, inconceivable till it happened. At that point, it became predictable, even inevitable.

There is, I note, an air of inevitability to events in the past. We can, for example, look at deepening European tensions and rivalries at the close of the Victorian Era, and declare the First World War a sure thing. But we're unable to defuse (or often, even recognize) the tensions that will touch off wars in our own future.

The people in this particular trap, Rock Creek Campground, were finished as soon as they pitched camp, just as surely as if they had been stood up against a wall and shot. Irrevocable, terrible natural law, passing sentence on anyone in the wrong place at the wrong time. All we frail humans can do is come in later, try to make sense of the mess, and as often as not, say, "Someone should have been prepared."

Then the thought hit me in a rush: that doesn't just apply to dolomite ridges or even such discrete human events as pitched wars. Culture itself is one more natural force, playing out mindlessly over eons. Psychological-sociological-behavioral patterns are predictable, there's a whole science around them.

I suddenly felt exquisitely uncomfortable, imagining the skeletons of those nineteen buried campers. Imagining the massive plates of earth's crust, our continent, creeping, sliding past one another so slowly we don't even know it's happening till a bunch of people get killed by another earthquake. But also imagining the genocide that spent hundreds of years creeping west out of Boston and Virginia and Savannah, destroying hundreds of First Nations, millions of human lives, as it went.

Change social viewpoint: were the human masses of Europe just another natural disaster waiting to happen, this one to North America, predictable to anyone with the right information and time to make the calculation?

Insight, to me, is a matter of accumulation, not genius. I had been moving toward this one all week without realizing it. Now that I did see it, it was so obvious I could hardly believe I hadn't always understood. Once those first boatloads of Europeans landed on North America's east coast, with their transportation and communication, their diseases and metallurgy and far-shooting weapons, indigenous lifeways were just as doomed as those campers. It took three centuries for the human earthquake to play out. But the crushing force of the European avalanche buried indigenous life just as inevitably as Rock Creek Campground got buried. Indigenous culture has been struggling to dig itself out of the rubble ever since.

Estimates vary widely, but say fifteen million people inhabited North America when Columbus arrived. Let's be optimistic and say two hundred fifty thousand indigenous people remained after four hundred years of European disease, war, land grab, starvation, and death from despair. That's quite an avalanche! Not that similar avalanches of genocide haven't played out plenty of other places, plenty of other times.

I grew up being told that humanity is the reasoning crown of creation. Looking at the broad sweep of things, though, I'm no longer convinced that we're any more self-aware than those two Columbian mammoths, locked in lust and mortal combat ten thousand years ago.

Days earlier, reflecting on those Minuteman Missile silos, I couldn't miss our culture's dance to the piping of evolving technology. It seems to me that we follow our inventions at least as often as we control them. Humbling.

What of individual human responsibility? My forbears just wanted to farm, not hurt anyone. Yet they were part and parcel to the Native American genocide, same as Custer. More appropriately, same as Vincent Charlie, dying in agony on his ridgetop in the fighting that, in Plenty Coups's words, broke the backs of the Lakota and Cheyenne.

I reflect on Plenty Coups, as well, and radical hope, survivance, and the subtle sense of commonality that led young Crow men to fight alongside Euro-Americans in World Wars I and II. To "give back" to the culture that had all but destroyed theirs. Is human nature wise enough to employ such wisdom *before* cultural devastation hits? I don't have answers to those questions.

I climbed back into my car and pulled back onto the highway. Driving back along Earthquake Lake, my feelings were like butterflies. Boy Scouts planted trees above Fort Robinson. Pretty Shield reared her granddaughters after their parents died of white people's diseases. The-Fringe saved a wounded Crow warrior and gained the love of his life. His right hand being irretrievably broken, White Swan used his left to paint exuberant scenes of hunts and battles he could never again join.

Radical hope does exist, and survivance. Victory, I reflected, lies in what's achievable, not in what's ideal.

HENRY'S FORK CALDERA

*S*outh of Hebgen Lake, the Montana-Idaho border follows the Continental Divide. I crossed the Continental Divide into Idaho the next day, Montana's Centennial Mountains towering as blue crenellations in my rear view mirror. The road leveled off, I entered the Henry's Fork Caldera. The jagged backs of the Grand Tetons loomed off to my left.

The Hebgen Lake earthquake didn't come out of nowhere. This whole region is a geological playground on a massive scale. The Henry's Fork Caldera is an immense volcanic crater, eighteen miles wide by twenty-three miles long. It marks a super eruption a million or so years ago, the mere crater of which matches the full swath of destruction produced by that volcanic popgun otherwise known as Mount St. Helens.

This eruption spewed out dozens of Mount St. Helens's worth of volcanic ash. Rich in iron and wonderfully fertile, the ash blanketed Idaho, Wyoming, Colorado, and a huge swath of the Great Plains. Such mega-eruptions are not singular incidents, but a sixteen-million-year series, carving their way across southern Idaho. The whole process is fueled by the Yellowstone Hot Spot, the column of molten magma that now throbs beneath Yellowstone Park.

That's just one living organ of our living planet. Tourists marvel at the geysers, hot springs, and boiling mud pots in Yellowstone Park itself, but those are just the current symptoms. That superheated rock has been cycling up thousands of miles from the earth's interior in a process that began long before humans even existed.

You wouldn't know it just by looking, though. I found myself driving through evergreen forest, dark and imperial on all sides. To my uneducated eye, the flat forest and wildflowers whisking past my windows embodied all the peace of a warm autumn day. I wouldn't have guessed at the roiling magma a thousand miles below my tires.

Whatever I may aspire to, I am definitely temporary. North America's slow process, a few centimeters a year, inching its way across this plume of magma, is too subtle for my sensing. The system blows sky-high every few hundred thousand years, or there's an earthquake, but it took centuries of scientific evolution for us to understand how it all fits together. Now we have instruments that measure the land as it rises and falls beneath Yellowstone Park, breathing, seething magma miles below our feet.

Twelve million years ago, the Bruneau-Jarbidge event buried those rhinos in eastern Nebraska and founded the loess hills of Iowa. Tomorrow, or perhaps a half million years from tomorrow, it will happen again. We scurry out our lives while geologic violence waits miles below our feet, like wrath from implacable gods, so slow motion we don't even know it's there.

On this day, though, the Henry's Fork Caldera welcomed me. That's what mattered. Autumn lay about me, mild and luxurious. Between the trees now and then, I glimpsed meanders of the Henry's Fork River itself. Fishing boats and water skiers played on broad reservoirs.

To me, there's a kind of spirituality somewhere in this mix. The autumn peace is real. The magma below our feet is real. The sun, multitudes of hydrogen bombs going off each instant, is also real. Each of us is a precious instant in the midst of it all.

HARRIMAN STATE PARK

*M*y next stop was a place called Harriman State Park, sited along an untrammeled stretch of the Henry's Fork River. The Henry's Fork flows into the Snake, which flows into the Columbia, which flows into the Pacific Ocean. This state park, I read, features some of the best fly fishing, cross-country skiing, bird watching, and just plain lazing about, in the world.

Harriman State Park's origins lay back in the nineteenth century "robber barons" era, when it was a sanctuary for ultra-rich business magnates. Edward Harriman, for whom it's named, was born the same year as Plenty Coups. Unlike Plenty Coups, Harriman's uncle worked for the New York Stock Exchange. Harriman also married well. By the time Plenty Coups was moving onto the reservation and trying to adjust to life in his square house, Harriman was buying and selling one railroad after another.

Late in his life, Plenty Coups traveled to Washington to lobby for Crow ownership of their own land. As chair of the Union Pacific and Southern Pacific Railroads, Harriman owned the rails over which Plenty Coups traveled. His freight trains carried Euro-American fortunes along the tracks past Crow Agency.

Harriman fell in love with the Henry's Fork country as a young man, spending his summers working at an iron furnace in the area. As his fortune grew, he bought land as it became available, and called his growing reserve the Railroad Ranch. It really was a working cattle ranch. After he died, it became the summer getaway for his descendants, as well as for the Guggenheim family, owners of American Smelting and Refining, and the Jones family of Atlantic Richfield. They could all train out to the mountains and enjoy nature far from the grimy masses. Railroad Ranch served about the same function as a baronial estate in Czarist Russia.

In 1977, the families donated the property to the state of Idaho as a waterfowl sanctuary. Just as Plenty Coups had done with his homestead thirty years before. It therefore seemed natural to me to follow up Chief Plenty Coups State Park with a tour of the magnates' old pleasure garden.

One more bouncy gravel turnoff, one more parking lot and visitors center. This place bustled with people. I walked past a "washing station." To keep fly anglers from accidentally carrying invasive organisms to the pristine Henry's Fork, they were required to disinfect their waders. And pristine those waters were. Walking paths led from vertical pine forest to a horizontal nirvana of yellow grasses, green cattails, and silver-blue water. I hadn't fly fished for thirty years, but it made my fingers itch just to see it.

I followed another path to the ranch house complex. It was really a campus, one rustic log building after another in a U shape, not unlike the old cavalry forts I had visited. Way more luxurious, though. As I entered one "cabin," a smiling docent in a flannel shirt handed me a complementary granola bar. Inside I found jaw-dropping rustic opulence. The only way I would have dared set foot in this place during the Railroad Ranch's heyday, was if they had hired me to install light fixtures.

Varnish gleamed on every inch of wood—and there were a lot of inches. Textured leather upholstery beckoned me to plant my fanny on a sofa and watch the console television, all styled mid twentieth-century. Books on built-in bookshelves, taffeta bedspreads, mud rooms, and picture windows which looked out over broad vistas of meadow and river.

I wondered for a moment what Plenty Coups would have done, had he magically been gifted with this spread. Plenty Coups did get invited to ride in parades, meet foreign dignitaries, and lay a Crow war bonnet and coup stick at the dedication of the Tomb of the Unknown Soldier. Photographs show the aged chieftain usually bemused by the foreign dignitaries and rituals swirling about him. He was the government's exhibit: how diverse and magnanimous we could be. The Harrimans, Guggenheims, and Joneses *owned* the government.

Far beyond the window in front of me, a breeze stippled the tranquil river. A thousand miles below my feet, the red-hot magma churned. It may wait another hundred human generations to burst forth again. Railroad Ranch will be buried, right along with everything else downwind.

SNAKE RIVER PLAIN

*I*n a photo taken from a weather satellite, the Snake
River Plain looks rather like a giant smiley face
stretched across southern Idaho. Created largely by blowouts
from the Yellowstone Hot Spot, it forms a corridor which
funnels Pacific moisture from Oregon's coast to the Grand
Tetons and Yellowstone Park highlands. There, forced higher
by the mountains, the moisture condenses and falls as rain
or snow.

The Tetons and Yellowstone Park receive moisture
appropriate to a rain forest. The Snake River Plain gets
hardly any. The ripe clouds proceed without stopping, "Do
not pass go, Do not collect $200."

The next day found me driving a blacktop ribbon across
the Snake River Plain, terrain that reminded me of the desert
valleys where I grew up. Mile after rolling mile of parched
ground, dotted here or there by struggling sage or grease
brush. Knobs of black basalt punctuated the landscape. It was
tinder and cinders all the way.

Yet this arid plain, I learned, was not as it seemed. A few
yards below me lay another underground lake, the Snake

River Aquifer. Subterranean basalt layers work as a perfect sponge, so you can't judge an aquifer by its cover. Rainfall in the mountains fed rivers that carved gorges, flowed toward the plain, then disappeared into the porous ground. Coupled with the region's loneliness and isolation, the underground water made it a perfect place to build—nuclear reactors.

Reading informed me that the eastern Snake River Plain is the nuclear research capital of the world. More than fifty nuclear reactors and research facilities, active and abandoned, checker the desert. I passed one side road after another, each guarded by a phalanx of threatening signage. "No Admittance to Unauthorized Personnel," one read. "For Admittance Return to Security Badging Office 5 Miles North." I could look down long driveways and see distant guard shacks, security fences, and massive square buildings. This was, I learned later, the Idaho National Laboratory, an evolving world of nuclear and military research. It's been growing like lichen out here ever since World War II. I grew up only a few hundred miles away, but never knew about it.

Working as an electrician in my thirties and forties, I spent years on construction crews at large electrical generating stations across the West, both coal-fired and nuclear. From an electricians-eye-view, there were surprising differences. Coal-fired power plants are huge, with extensive coal-handling facilities, mountains of coal waiting to be crushed and burned, and massive "scrub" facilities to filter toxic particulates and gases out of the smoke. Thousands of tons of coal are brought in over miles of roads and railroad tracks. Miles of conveyor belts haul the ash away, to be dumped in park-sized tailings ponds.

The first thing that struck me working at a "nuke" was how small it was. No coal-handling, no ash disposal. Even the reactor building, where the nuclear core heated water to drive the steam turbine generator, was tiny compared to a coal-fired boiler. Much more strongly built, though, with walls of thick, double-steel reinforced concrete. Keeping electricians like me busy, there were also double the power cable and control wiring, all layered into much smaller spaces. Another inconvenience, from my point of view, was the full week of nuclear safety training we had to go through before they would even let us walk through the gate.

SMALL SPACES

*T*he terrain I now drove across could have been moonscape if not for distant mountains—and mile after mile of American nuclear research. My destination was a red square marked on my map, "EBR-1 Nat'l Hist. Landmark." This, I had learned, was a sanctum of nuclear history, America's first "Atoms for Peace" experimental breeder reactor.

Atoms for Peace was the brainchild of President Dwight Eisenhower's administration back in the 1950s. Nuclear research and development were immense, not just the Snake River plain, but facilities the size of cities sprouting all across the country. Given twenty first-century cynicism toward institutions, particularly federal programs, it's easy to forget the enthusiasm for nuclear energy in those early days. The Manhattan Project and Atoms for Peace were viewed as wonderful without mitigation.

While nuclear energy's benevolence seemed unlimited, uranium fuel was thought to be rare. No one foresaw deposits like Crow Butte, let alone the technology to exploit them. Thus the breeder reactor, to maximize the small amount of nuclear fuel we thought we had.

Surround a core of enriched U-235 with a blanket of non-radioactive U-238. Surplus atomic particles from the core provoke a secondary reaction in the surrounding material. This creates radioactive byproducts, both usable and unusable.

Beginning serious operation in 1951, EBR-1 was the first attempt to do this for peaceful purposes. Physicists at the time considered it a raging success. They conducted experiments on fuel, cooling agents, procedures, and reactor dynamics. As it gave rise to new research facilities, of course, EBR-1 became obsolete. It was deactivated in 1964, declared a historical landmark in 1965, and is now a museum.

Driving that direction, I became used to forbidding signage, long access roads, and miles of perimeter fencing. EBR-1 sat at the end of one such approach. If I found commercial nuclear power plants small compared to coal-fired ones, this place was just plain tiny. It looked like a warehouse with attitude, or perhaps a cross between a high school and a prison. It was surrounded by more fencing, flanked by a guard shack, office annex, and cooling structures.

The shady interior even felt like walking into the basement of that high school, into something like an oversized utility room. Except for the banks of control panels, museum-style interpretive displays, and the angular containment structure in the middle. People quietly read the displays or mused over the bulky mid-twentieth-century electronics. A few whispered to each other. I think they were experiencing the same mixed emotions I was: awe mitigated by time-warp.

The utopian vision of this 1950s flashback felt strange, compared to the nuclear energy controversies of our day.

During my childhood we were chauvinistically proud of our scientists and technicians. It was the cutting edge of human ingenuity and we believed the United States owned it. EBR-1 required two years of construction, installation, and tweaking of nuclear reactions to produce its first triumph. Engineers succeeded in illuminating four 200-watt light bulbs.

A docent explained to us that there wasn't much on-site celebration at the time. The scientists were so worn out from their months of hard work, they just went home thinking, Thank God that's done. A display photograph showed the beaming crew, proudly posing with that string of bare, incandescent bulbs.

I walked past the generator. Again, if commercial nuclear power stations are small compared to coal-fired ones, this was infinitesimal. The backup generators I've seen in commercial buildings are larger than this one was.

It was a success, though, including "breeding" nuclear fuel. They learned a lot about cooling materials, too. This reactor was cooled by an alloy of sodium and potassium, called "nacky" after its atomic symbol, NaK. Both are so-called alkali metals, liquid at or near room temperature.

I later learned sodium and sodium-potassium coolants had real advantages over water-cooled reactor cores. Later experiments at EBR-I's descendant, EBR-II, even showed that a sodium-cooled reactor could suffer a total, Fukushima-style loss of coolant circulation and shut itself down without mishap.

Alas, both elements are among the most volatile known. They are difficult to keep in containment, burn on contact with air, and explode on contact with water. Authorities at the time considered them too dangerous for use in full-scale nuclear power production.

Among other projects spawned by EBR-1 was an experimental reactor called BORAX-III. In 1955 they hooked that one up to the electrical grid in the Idaho town of Arco, a few miles away. That made Arco the first town powered by nuclear-generated electricity. It was, I read, a huge deal at the time, celebrated with speeches and ceremony. There's still a commemorative "Atoms for Peace" marker along US Highway 20, where it runs west out of Arco.

Looking back at photos or watching taped interviews, the scientists' excitement, sense of teamwork, and joy of success are palpable. They were devoted professionals at the cutting edge of human creativity. It felt slightly odd to look back after decades of fine print and debate on nuclear power. This is a perfect example of what I call creativity's shadow side. We developed truly amazing technology, only to spawn the threat of globe-destroying nuclear war on one side, and environmental damage we'll spend the next century cleaning up on the other.

Even in those joyful early days, there were unpleasant surprises. BORAX-III's reactor core was only the size of a household water heater. But while testing coolant procedures in 1955, trying to understand unexpected heat surges, they accidentally overheated it and melted part of the core itself. Luckily, it was surrounded by a steel-and-concrete housing, so damage was minimal. No one got hurt, nothing got destroyed, and the supervisor noted that a great deal was learned.

Another experiment down the road, Stationary Low-Power Reactor #1 (SL-1), wasn't as lucky. SL-1 was a small, prototype reactor designed for actual power generation. The plan was to mass produce these things, then ship them to remote locations as pre-fab nuclear power generators. SL-1 was water cooled because that was thought safer and easier to use than the NaK cooling compound.

They started it up in 1958 and it ran fine for a couple of years. But in January 1960, after a routine maintenance shut-down, three workers were preparing it for re-start. It seems incredible today, but part of that process was to manually re-attach the reactor control rods to the automatic lifting system. Looking back, the procedure for doing that—well, breathtakingly Mickey Mouse is the term that springs to my mind.

Each control rod had to be hand lifted, using a clumsy vertical handle. It was then *C-clamped* into place while the automated lifting linkage was bolted up. C-clamped? A nuclear reactor? Are they kidding me? Topping that off, to accomplish this, the technicians had to stand on top of the reactor housing itself.

I suppose I need to be humble, here. We don't know what we don't know until we learn it. And sometimes we learn the hard way. Two generations of hindsight can make something look abysmally stupid when, at the time, it seemed quite acceptable. I remind myself to reflect now and then on what people fifty-five years from now might say about my generation's lapses.

Still, looking back, it seems as though they were asking for it. And they got it. No one knows why, but the workers lifted the assembly too far. There's still argument on how and why this happened. The resultant explosion didn't leave enough evidence for investigators to sort out the details.

Some investigators proposed that it was deliberate suicide. Or perhaps the control rod stuck in the housing and the workers were trying to jerk it free. There seems to be no *likely* explanation, which has to mean that something unlikely happened. There's the shadow side of creativity again. How do you prepare for what you can't foresee?

Whatever the reason, instead of lifting the control rod four inches, they jerked it up twenty inches. The nuclear fuel went into an uncontrolled "excursion" state. The U-235 core melted in less than a second, vaporized the water coolant, and the steam exploded. The whole containment vessel took off like a rocket, bounced off the overhead beams, then bounced back onto its foundation.

Fired like a bullet from a gun, one control rod hit the overhead, shattered, and shot broken pieces all over the chamber. Another control rod shot up, pierced one technician from groin to shoulder, and pinned him to the ceiling. I can only hope death came quickly. Another man was instantly scalded to death by steam and radiation. The third lasted about an hour. To this day, these three remain the only people killed by a nuclear accident in the United States. That strikes me as a big "only."

Because of radiation, it took days for men working in one-minute shifts to retrieve the bodies. They buried the victims in lead caskets encased in concrete. Except, I read, for "certain body parts," which had to be treated as radioactive waste. The rest of the reactor structure was broken down to the ground piece-by-piece, and also treated as radioactive waste. They buried all those pieces in the empty desert.

Needless to say, the Atomic Energy Commission reviewed procedures and scrapped this design. The official attitude was, this was "an industrial accident," and industrial accidents will happen. I guess that's true as far as it goes.

Looking at Japan's Fukushima Daiichi accident, we've learned that in the immensity of time, there's always one more unforeseen event. One more "industrial accident" waiting to happen.

Wandering through the successful EBR-1 museum, though, I couldn't get over how joyous and innocent nuclear research seemed at the time. The scientists in those photos are so filled with pride. The positive energy they got from their cutting-edge research, hard work, and accomplishment, practically leap off the paper. I also have to humbly ask, despite the ghastliness of SL-1, or even the financial and social carnage of Fukushima Daiichi, how does this stack up against hundreds of deaths each year related to the coal-fired electrical power industry?

I don't have answers to such questions. More to the point, I doubt that's even the right question. Is the energy source the real problem, or does the problem lie in the energy users? Does the onus lie on the people who sell us what we want: hot stoves, cool air conditioners, microwaves, bright lights, flat-screen televisions? Or should it really lie on the people who buy those things?

We can add hundreds of nuclear accidents, of varying degrees, to the hundreds of nuclear weapon "broken arrows" over the decades. On the other hand, numbers of cable TV infotainment series have been produced around nothing but the many ways every kind of technology has gone wrong. It's not just nuclear weapons or power plants. Hundreds of oil refinery blow outs, millions of computer glitches, millions of so-called electronic "tin whiskers" which cause complex systems to go awry. Many deaths, much destruction, it all turns out to be predictably unpredictable.

If I believed in an afterlife, I might imagine the spirit of Plenty Coups. "The white man . . . is like a god in some ways but foolish—foolish—in others. He fools nobody but himself."

While I'm at it, though, lest I seem overly romantic about Plenty Coups's wisdom, Pretty Shield tells a story where the wise chief accidentally discharged his rifle during a religious celebration, killing a woman in his own village. It's not about who's wiser, which is probably all of us at one time or another. It's about who's fallibly human and how each of us can be fooled by our own innovation. That's the spirit I was finding, thick as a dust storm on the Snake River Plain.

HEAT TRANSFER

*A*s I walked to my car after viewing the EBR-1 Museum, my eyes lit on two immense structures that towered over one end of the parking lot. Referring again to my construction-worker past, the rusting I-beams, tangled ductwork, and electrical circuitry, all wrapped around central, tank-like objects, reminded me of pieces ripped out of an old oil refinery. I saw an interpretive display nestled between them and had to investigate. The structures were, of all things, nuclear-powered jet airplane engines!

It turns out that when World War II ended and the cold war began, our military wanted ways to deliver nuclear warheads over the Soviet Union. An atom bomb weighed a good five tons in those days, which called for bombers of unprecedented size and speed. Jet engines were in their infancy. It didn't seem outlandish to imagine nuclear-powered bombers fast enough to outrun jet fighter planes and able to stay on patrol for weeks at a time.

My eyebrows lifted, but there the damned things were, right in front of me. Studying the diagrams and the structures themselves, I could make out the ductwork to two old jet engines. Later reading informed me that they were J47s, one of the first successful jet engine designs. The big tank in the middle was the reactor. The two structures were "Heat Transfer Reactor Experiments," numbers 2 and 3.

Scientists labored fifteen years on this project. The final version, HTRE-3, used radioactive fluoride salt as fuel, housed the reaction within a beryllium oxide container, and cooled it with liquid sodium. The process superheated air, which was then ducted into the jet engines. Crazy though it sounds, the thing got built. And they ran it for thousands of hours.

The Air Force adapted a B-36 bomber to accept the contraption. The B-36 was another postwar oddity, a huge bomber driven by six propellers, designed to carry those five-ton, first-generation atom bombs. Jet engine advances soon made the B-36 obsolete, so it was never used. But it was the perfect platform for testing a nuclear jet engine.

This struck me as the perfect example of how wild early nuclear research got. Also what a dead end looks like. But we were willing to pour billions of dollars into such dead ends. While this work was going on, other scientists were developing smaller, more efficient thermonuclear devices. Missile technology was racing forward. By the late 1950s, nuclear powered aircraft had become superfluous. Not to mention way too expensive to be practical.

We spent three million dollars on the EBR-1 reactor, which resulted in nuclear breakthroughs all around the world. Whether I love atomic power or hate it, I can't argue that we got our three million bucks worth of value from that investment.

We spent fifteen *billion* dollars on the Heat Transfer Reactor Experiments. Back when a billion bucks was worth almost ten times what it is now. Then, after listening to the experts, President John Kennedy canceled the thing in 1961.

I mused on the tubing, steel, and rust towering above me, the artist's conception of an operational nuclear airplane, the rusting test reactors, and of course another platoon of beaming scientists posing in front of their successful experiment. I can't think of a better nutshell into which to put the human dilemma. War and rumors of war brought energy and inventiveness unmatched by all other endeavors. Ask for a cure for Alzheimer's, we get a grant here and there, but mostly crickets. But look for a way to bomb Russia and we threw tons of billions of dollars at it. Hardly anyone complained at the time, not least because hardly any civilian knew we were even doing it.

None of this nuclear energy research turned out the way we expected it to back in the 1950s. Our missiles still sit in their silos, even though we know it's crazy. We now look at active nuclear power plants more as environmental menaces than efficient producers of needed energy. We watch our climate grow warmer every year while all too many people still pretend they don't see unprecedented hurricanes, wildfires, and green lawns in January.

We spend billions of dollars to beat swords into plowshares, or beat plowshares into swords. We'll all be generations dead and gone before anyone knows whether we bought something or just threw our money away, or even whether we wound up with a plowshare or a sword. We till fields broad beyond our vision: prisoners, rather than masters, of our creativity. I climbed back into my car and drove away from this strange monument on the empty desert, with its buried bodies and rusting dreams.

CINDERS AS FAR AS THE EYE
CAN SEE

*W*hile I explored the Snake River Plain's nuclear research memorials, I camped at Craters of the Moon National Monument. Again, looking at a weather satellite photo, the Snake River Plain forms a curving band of tan and green, fading to gray where the volcanic track of the Yellowstone Hotspot comes in. Against those muted colors, Craters of the Moon's black lava fields stick down from the north like a sore thumb.

The eruptions began through a seventy-five-mile crack in the earth's crust, back in the days of the Columbian mammoth. Lava spewed for thousands of years, finally ceasing while the first Caesars ruled Rome. The cinders have long cooled. Now they stretch as far as the eye can see, a thousand square miles of blasted desert.

Big as that sounds, it was just a sideshow. The Yellowstone Hotspot's really huge blowouts wiped out whole ecosystems half a continent away. This only scabbed over a chunk of the Idaho desert. There's huge, then there's really huge. Then there's so big you run out of adjectives.

Put this in context? An area called the Siberian Traps, in

northern Russia, consists of lava flows a *mile* deep across *millions* of square miles. The earth belched lava and sulfur dioxide gas continuously for a *million* years back in the Archeozoic. It wiped out 96 percent of all life on earth. Only the very strongest species survived the poisonous, world-wide haze. On the bright side, that mass extinction opened the door for the age of dinosaurs, and much later, us. Death equals life. Life equals change. Change equals—I don't know where this equation leads.

So I stood one morning on the highway pullout above Craters of the Moon, looking to the black horizon of this finite volcanic sideshow. I felt pretty finite myself. One life form on a small planet in a moderate solar system in one of billions of galaxies.

At such moments, I have a hard time buying what some folks call the "anthropic principle," or even Carl Sagan's "We are the universe coming to know itself." At our best, we do struggle to know the universe. What we really come to know is the painfully counterintuitive reality that what we learn is bigger than what we are. And we grow tinier with every new insight.

We're not the center of creation, nor the measure of all things. The meaning we make is the meaning we are. We struggle and survive and love and bring forth new life and new love. In our heedlessness, we too often destroy. When all's said and done, it seems to me, we have one another and the living things around us. When we're gone, if we screw up and get ourselves gone the way those two Columbian mammoths in Nebraska got themselves gone, the universe will not remember us, nor even mark our passing. Even the earth will barely notice.

I find that not depressing, but reverence-inspiring. I also find it a humbling kick in the pants toward taking the long view. If our Nth-generation great-grandchildren matter, it's on us to try to be nurse logs rather than heedless eaters of life. Reverence—religion—blesses us with this challenge: to nurture a future in which humanity still flourishes. I don't know if we're up for that challenge. I hope we are. As our world shifts around us, I suspect we'll get a closer look at Jonathan Lear's take on radical hope than we expect or want.

Or to put it a slightly different way, my own brain and body consist of myriad, wonderful, interlocked systems. We're still learning the intricacies. Yet it's just one of billions of bodies, each tiny almost beyond measurement compared to the vastness of the cosmos. That's wonderful in itself, also inspiring of a multi-layered awe.

Meanwhile, for all its geologic violence, our earth is still a relatively gentle planet in a gentle sector of the Milky Way Galaxy. So we're challenged to somehow embrace life on this gentle-but-occasionally-lethal planet of ours, with its eminently non-gentle, carbon-based life forms. Back to the challenge of the religious life. I'll love and lift your tiny humanity if you'll love and lift mine. How much more do we have?

My eye strayed back from the horizon and lit on a tuft of vegetation growing from a crack between volcanic boulders. At first it seemed incongruous that a wildflower could struggle up from such barrenness. A couple thousand years of dust must have settled into the bottom of that crack to support it. And a seed blew in. A sprinkle of rain now and then, and seeds have no choice but to try to grow wherever they land.

Lava fields are incredibly rugged terrain. Traveling off designated walkways is prohibited, but even if a person tried, basalt edges sharp as broken glass would quickly cut even the stoutest shoes to ribbons. Yet everywhere I wandered, grasses and wildflowers sprouted from fissures and low places. It might take thousands more years, but they are going to show the harsh stone who's boss. There, it seems to me, is a lesson in survivance.

It struck me like a flash: T.S. Eliot was wrong, April is *not* the cruelest month, breeding flowers from the dead land. Flowers breeding from the dead land is an act of heroism which merits deep human reverence. Ever and always, P-Tr Extinction Event or these lava fields or whatever the backside of human technology may do to us, life will ever venture forth upon the blasted land.

If we want the meaning of life, far as I'm concerned, there it is. Human greatness, I say, is a delusion. Achievement is just a spark against the relentless winds and limitless tides of time and change. But a seed drills into new soil, a hand is offered to a new stranger. As long as our species endures, that will be the meaning and achievement that matters. "Once you are dead," the artist said, "all the differences of this world are not important."

FUJITARO KUBOTA

*I*t's late summer, 1942, a hot, dry day in southern Idaho.
A railroad track winds along the Snake River's broad
flood plain, and a passenger train squeaks onto a siding. The riders
are grimy with dust and coal smoke because they kept the windows
open to get what breeze they could.

They are Americans of Japanese descent—"internees." Pursuant
to President Franklin D. Roosevelt's Executive Order 9066, they
have been assigned to one of eleven "relocation centers" across the
American West. This presidential order was not debated in
congress. It was barely even discussed at the White House. It is
heedless cruelty of the first order: a quick conversation rooted in
bigotry, a scratch of pen on paper, and people suffer for years as a
result.

"Our" government (that is, the government of people who look
like me) assumes that because of their facial features, Japanese
American businessmen, housewives, artists, and children are
"threats to national security" in the war against Japan. A stain of
racist madness bleeds through the order's bureaucratic language.
Japanese Americans are not being detained in Hawaii or east of the

Mississippi. Executive Order 9066 applies only to Japanese Americans along the West Coast.

They were evicted from their homes and businesses on a few hours' notice. They have the clothes on their backs plus what each person could cram into a single suitcase. Nothing else. No one has bothered to tell them where they are or where they are going.

A hot breeze stirs the passenger car curtains. Soldiers with bayonets order the people out, then line them up along the siding. A few whisper to one another as the soldiers count them. Tears trace their way down a few faces, and women keep small children close to them, refusing to let go of little hands. Some wonder if they are about to be shot.

Buses approach, throwing up more dust. They grind to a stop and the soldiers order the people in. Then it's off across the basalt-strewn desert to pull up in front of what looks like a prison work farm. A guard tower, constructed of bare timbers, looms over them. Guards with rifles look down. There's a wart-ugly stone guardhouse built from the black basalt, which seems to lie everywhere.

Guards check identifications and herd the people through the barbed wire gate. Before them stand three miles of tarpaper barracks, forty-four blocks of asphalt roofs and bare wood interiors. Each structure is divided into three "rooms" by panels which do not go all the way to the ceiling. Each room has a wood-burning stove and three cots with straw mattresses. There is no plumbing. Each room will house one complete family, parents and children. The cots are the only furniture.

This is where they will endure the next three years. They will eventually make tables and chairs from old packing crates and cast-off wood. It's not Dachau because the ground is too rocky and dry to be Dachau. It's not Guantanamo because it hardly ever rains here. The people will eventually be released to restart their lives. But it is definitely a concentration camp. A hundred thousand Japanese Americans will spend the rest of the war in camps like this one.

They will be allowed to play music, dance, make lives here in whatever ways they can devise. Adults will be sent to work on farms because so many white workers are off fighting the war. (The same way camp labor is used in Birkenau and Treblinka I, except the Japanese internees get more food, plus straw to sleep on.) Children will attend camp schools, where they will be ordered to place their hands over their hearts and pledge allegiance to America's flag "with liberty and justice for all." Only later will the children appreciate the irony of that ritual.

The young men will be invited to enlist in the US Army. More than a thousand will, from this one camp alone. They will be required to promise to fight loyalty for the United States, and also forswear their loyalty to the Emperor of Japan. Which is precisely like asking General Dwight D. Eisenhower to forswear his loyalty to Adolf Hitler. Those who name the ridiculousness of the loyalty pledges and refuse to comply will be imprisoned for "Draft Evasion." Those who do comply and serve will be formed into so-called Nisei Regiments. They will be the most decorated soldiers of the Second World War, with the highest casualty rates. In slack moments, they will write letters home to their parents, still detained in America's concentration camps.

As a friend of mine once put it, human nature can consist of ingratitude on two legs.

This is not an abstract exercise. These were real people with real lives. In 1942, operating one of the most successful nursery and garden businesses on the West Coast, Fujitaro Kubota and his family were sent from their home in Seattle to the Minidoka Relocation Center. They took the train ride, lined up along the siding in their good shoes, then rode the bus. With tears visible or invisible, they stared through the door into the single room which would house all four of them for the next four years.

Like the others, they created life there as best they could. For his part, Fujitaro Kubota did what he did best. In his spare hours, he created a traditional Japanese garden outside their tarpaper barrack. When he was not cultivating sugar beets for the white farmers, he gathered interesting stones and desert plants. He used leftovers from camp construction to build a terrace, artistry against the desert's harsh tedium. He pursued his specialty, combining local plants with Japanese gardening traditions. On reflection, I see this as what survivance looked like for one interned Japanese American in the 1940s.

When the camp was closed, the family was given twenty-five dollars and a bus ticket, then allowed to return to Seattle and start over. Years abandoned, Kubota Gardens was in disarray. They resolutely set about reweaving the fabric of their lives.

Fujitaro Kubota kept some of the lava stone from Minidoka, particularly a one-ton section of lava tube, which he later had shipped to Seattle and used to build a garden at his private residence. In a YouTube video, his granddaughter tells how he wouldn't talk much about these stones, only that they came from "the camp." He got angry when she touched them once. That's how she learned "the camp" was a bad memory.

The remains of Mr. Kubota's garden at Minidoka fell into disrepair. Local Japanese citizens later restored the old stones as part of the historic site. Human nature can also consist of forgiveness on two legs, and resolve to leave the past in the past. That strikes me as a mighty thing, requiring real strength.

MINIDOKA

From Craters of the Moon, I had to search a network of obscure Idaho back roads to find Minidoka National Historic Site. I passed trucks loaded with Idaho potatoes or huge sugar beets. Sometimes called Magic Valley, this part of the Snake River plain is surprisingly fertile, due to windblown loam and high iron content from all those volcanic eruptions.

I finally found a gravel side road flanked by two historical markers. One told about the fossils of early mammals found in this area, along with campsites of ten thousand-year-old hunters. The other commemorated "Hunt Relocation Camp." That, I learned, was the place name favored by locals. "Until they could resettle in other places, they lived in wartime tarpaper barracks," it read, "in a dusty desert, where they helped meet a local farm labor crisis, planting and harvesting crops."

It sounded all too innocent to me. No concentration camp, just temporary wartime lodging, right? The text did go on to say, "Finally, a 1945 Supreme Court decision held that

United States citizens no longer could be confined that way, and their camp became Idaho's largest ghost town."

Interesting paragraph, I thought, both for what it said and for what it didn't say. I wondered whether its clunkiness rose from compromise between Japanese American citizen groups who wanted the story told, versus local politicians who didn't. That was just my guess.

The road wound along a broad irrigation canal. On the other side, outcroppings of volcanic basalt poked up through the sagebrush. Crushed basalt gravel covered the road's surface, dark and gritty. It was only a short drive before I pulled up at the abandoned camp. I could hear the nearby murmuring of the canal's waters as I got out.

I've visited another such site, the Topaz Internment Site in central Utah, where nothing is left but a plaque and the concrete pads where the buildings once stood. Here, a few walls still stood, being constructed from the ubiquitous basalt. What the two camps had in common, and in common with other internment sites I've seen in photographs, is the forbidding starkness of the land itself. They were built on waste land, nothing to offer except hot summers, cold winters, dust, and bugs.

Wandering through the interpretive displays, I once again felt conflicting emotions. I've heard a generation of white Americans argue that the internment was a crime and a travesty on American values. Incredible as it sounds, though, I have heard others, even relatives, say with a straight face that it was necessary for the Japanese Americans' own good. To protect them.

Looking about, I felt sad and angry. That we could have done this, or that any American would justify it a generation later. Or worst of all, that we seem quite capable of doing it again in our own time, to Americans of Middle Eastern or Hispanic descent, or whatever descent happens, in the moment, to be deemed sufficiently threatening. Such clue-lessness. Injustice. Heartbreak.

Barely flickering through that curtain, though, I also felt that same gleam of admiration I got at Chief Plenty Coups's homestead and the Native Memorial at the Little Bighorn Battlefield. It occurs to me, when we human beings are most foul to one another, resistance can be no more than a song sung, a prayer uttered, a dance danced, or a Japanese garden built on basalt terraces. Those, too, can be flowers breeding out of the dead land. There's a subtlety to survivance, which I believe we of the dominant culture would do well to study.

Suffering and injustice are often big, I reflect again, and triumph is often small and subtle. This human spirit requires an eye for nuance.

PLUTONIUM

*I*n my motel room, my laptop cast shadowy light on my face. I wryly suspected I looked like an actor in an old horror movie. I was reading about plutonium, a human-made metal first synthesized in 1940. Plutonium is easily oxidized. It's silvery gray like lead, but heavier and much harder. A golfball-size piece of plutonium weighs more than two pounds. If someone tried to saw that piece of plutonium in half, it would quickly wear out the hacksaw blade. Best not to try, though. The dust is radioactive, also poisonous. If ingested, it heads straight to bones. Snap a few of those golf balls together fast, there's a hell of an explosion. In short, plutonium is way-dangerous stuff, on multiple levels.

To make weapons-grade plutonium requires a breeder process, bombarding U-238 with neutrons from a U-235 reaction. Sadly, we were using nuclear reactors to build plutonium bombs years before we learned to generate electricity with one. Even more sadly, every ounce of weapons-grade plutonium also results in many ounces of deadly byproducts, all of which have to be stored somewhere. Plutonium is the ultimate gift that keeps on giving. In the worst possible way.

Driving west out of Idaho the next morning, I took Interstate 84 northwest, across the corner of Oregon, up into eastern Washington, toward the Columbia River. I crossed that broad stream, sped up a range of low hills, and paused at the crest to take in the view. Grassland sprawled as far as the eye could see, fading to the horizon in dusty haze.

In this part of Washington, the Columbia River comes down from the north, bends a three-quarter circle, joins the Yakima and Snake Rivers, and heads toward the Pacific Ocean. The plain within that loop, bounded on three sides by river, is called Hanford Reach. It was, for two generations, the plutonium-making capital of the world. At its south edge lie the towns of Kennewick and Richland, my next destination.

Breeder reactors require huge quantities of water for cooling. Back in the 1940s, that made this loop of river the pivot point of the Manhattan Project. The first reactor there, called B-Reactor, still stands at the northern end.

B-Reactor is the one breeder reactor whose plutonium was used in anger, taking lives. A lot of lives. Some of the scientists who created those bombs, among them J. Robert Oppenheimer himself, were aghast at what they had done. Then the arms race escalated and we built another breeder reactor. Then another. By cold war's end, nine huge structures brooded in a great arc along the Columbia, cranking out plutonium in industrial quantities. Along with tons of radioactive and toxic waste.

The reactors produced superheated water, which got dumped back into the river. Rising water temperatures were bad for fish and wildlife. The indigenous Nez Perce and Yakima people, some of whom had been shooed away when the government claimed the land, protested as damage to the fishery became obvious. Now, a generation later, some reactors have been torn down. Others still loomed in the distance, like cyclopean temples to runaway technology. B-Reactor was one. It was shut down in 1968, but survives as a museum. Alas, reservations to tour the B-Reactor museum must be booked months in advance. The downside of my follow-my-nose journey was that I would only be able to view B-reactor from a distance.

I followed two-lane blacktop twenty miles up the Reach's west side, re-crossed the Columbia, and pulled off at a viewpoint. A historical marker there had been shot full of bullet holes by gun-toting vandals, but I could still read it. A diagram laid out B-Reactor and explained its workings.

On the positive side, as the government shut down breeder reactors, the prairie around the complex became Hanford Reach National Monument. On the negative side, the Hanford Site is one of the most toxic places in the world. It holds two-thirds of all American nuclear waste, the radioactive risk of which is hard to conceptualize. The financial cost of chemical processing and permanent storage has been even harder to conceptualize.

Reading news articles from B-Reactor's "salad days," little concern was expressed about cleaning it up later. It was all about winning World War II, then about winning the arms race that followed. It was, for decades, unpatriotic to criticize our nuclear defense industry.

The enriched uranium for those breeder reactors came first from Oak Ridge, Tennessee, then from additional enrichment sites at Paducah, Kentucky, and Portsmouth, Ohio. They're all toxic cleanup sites now, on an unbelievable scale, with Hanford as the focal point of it all.

We "enriched" Uranium-238 by a method called gaseous diffusion. Looking back seventy years, it's an amazing feat of chemistry, at least to this non-scientist. A string of chemical processes produced a gaseous compound, uranium hexafluoride. The gas was then forced through a series of filters, separating out enough U-238 to increase the percentage from about .7 per cent to about 5 per cent. That may not sound like much difference, but it means everything.

The catch was, the process generated nearly a million tons of so-called DUF6, the depleted uranium hexafluoride left over from enrichment. DUF6 is highly unstable. Expose it to air and it breaks down into a nightmare list of toxic poisons and acids. Not that the nuclear industry was unique in producing poison. Through the post-World War II decades, we realized too slowly a range of industrial activities was producing mountains of toxic waste. It crept up on us, hidden by our excitement at the wonders we were creating.

The Hanford site strikes me as emblematic of all that. Complex and expensive, cleanup will go on for at least another generation. Sixty million gallons of waste lie in dozens of underground steel tanks. Because it's so much nastier than anyone realized in the 1950s, we must now retreat and re-dispose of the entire mess. The plan is to melt it into glass, then confine it in steel canisters which we will bury to a harmless depth. We hope. Total cost, perhaps seventy-five billion dollars. That's three-quarters of the cost of the Vietnam War. That's Hanford alone.

It now turns out the problem is even worse than that. The contractor in charge spent a year denying that the old holding tanks had begun to leak radioactive sludge. But the leakage has now been confirmed. Now both the government and the contractor must extensively revise their plans. At appropriately added cost and time.

I stood and gazed across the Columbia River's broad waters at buildings where, for decades, death was quietly manufactured in bulk. It was a luscious, warm autumn day, a bit of a breeze. It all looked so innocent. It wasn't just the banality of evil, I reflected, it was more complex than that. It was the backside of creativity itself. We most prize our human ability to innovate. But these particular innovations led us into dangers few recognized until the fish started to die and the drinking water turned to poison.

THE REACH

$\mathcal{I}$ spent the next morning at the new museum dedicated to Hanford Reach National Monument and the Columbia River. It was a crisp, prairie-colored building overlooking the Columbia's broad flow. Wild grasses swayed in plantings, the asphalt of the parking lot was black and new. I was the first person there that morning.

A tall, white-haired gentleman, slightly stooped of shoulder, greeted me. "Volunteer," his name tag read. Enthusiastically pressing information brochures into my hand, he reminded me of the nice lady at Fort Robinson, showing me their Columbian mammoth. "Hell of a nice guy," I thought to myself. He smiled as he showed me around, and I couldn't resist smiling back.

He was just as proud of the new museum as she was of the mammoth, and I couldn't blame him. Soft light bathed gleaming galleries, displays interactive and ingenious. He showed me lava flows in action, and prehistoric fang and claw. Where I lost myself, though, was the Manhattan Project Gallery.

Storyboards, charts, and graphics described the massive

enterprise. Sixty thousand people flooded into the Hanford Reach, it announced: scientists, engineers, construction workers, and their families. They built towns, formed communities, and erected sprawling research complexes all over this inland peninsula. In just a couple years, they built the core of our nuclear weapons industry.

Only later would our nuclear dream come true turn out to be a nightmare. We awoke to international paranoia, duck-and-cover drills, radioactive mutation stories, and the creeping pessimism of a new and troubled age. I watched Hollywood, which I view as America's subconscious, process our nuclear fears through my childhood and after: *Them*, *Godzilla*, *Atomic Age Vampire*, *On the Beach*, *Planet of the Apes*, tapering into *Mad Max*, curling around *Blade Runner*, spreading through *The Hunger Games*. B-Reactor was the wedge end of a new, dystopian outlook in popular culture. The Manhattan Project's creators didn't see that coming at first, either.

One display consisted of simple statistics, scribed onto 1940s-era, 78 RPM phonograph records, glued to a huge photo of two people jitterbugging in front of a jukebox. Thousands of transplanted families lived in thousands of hastily gathered mobile homes. "The world's largest trailer park," it read. They smoked sixteen thousand packages of cigarettes each day. They gulped down seven hundred cases of Coca-Cola. Each week, they ate one hundred thirty-five tons of meat. Fewer than 1 percent of them knew exactly what they were making. They just knew their project was supposed to win the war.

Another display framed the story in terms of saving lives. Invading Japan would bring a million Allied casualties, it read. A mere two destroyed cities, particularly *their* cities, not ours, was a nice alternative. A generation accepted that reasoning, at least on our side of the Pacific. Slowly though, even in the United States, debate began. Was it *really* necessary to drop—not one, but two—atomic bombs in the summer of 1945? The debate has gone on ever since.

I don't see it being resolved in my lifetime. But I have come to doubt that's even the point. Hardly anything about nuclear power turned out the way anyone expected, even for those most "in the know." It was just one more time we reached through the veil of human creativity, ignorant of all we might draw out. We *thought* we knew, of course. We always seem to *think* we know what we're setting loose. Then we realize that the future, abetted by our own cleverness, has played bait-and-switch on us.

Looking at the displays, though, these were families of such *nice* people. They were nice people in the same way my guide was a nice person, friendly, enthusiastic, proud of what they were doing. No one mentioned the shadow.

Unlike the internees at Minidoka, they drew good pay, got to drink soda pop and eat steak, didn't have to worry about getting shot, and could pursue their dreams and be called "good" by the rest of society. Now we'll spend my children's generation and the next cleaning up the damage they created. If it can be cleaned up.

Meanwhile, the museum docent was such a nice man, and his enthusiasm for The Reach's exhibits was so infectiously enthusiastic. When I finished my wandering, I made it a point to pass his counter on the way out, thank him and shake his hand. Because no human being is omniscient. Not me, not him, not the human beings who created the Hanford Site. We need to call one another to accountability, but not despise one another because of what a person does not yet understand. That balance is more easily described than practiced. We need to return the kindnesses we receive, I say, even as we grieve the fact that kindness alone will not secure a livable future.

RAINIER

From Hanford Reach, broad and beige, US Highway 12 led up the winding Yakima River and into the towering Cascade Mountains. Another hour found me driving between slopes dark with evergreens.

The Cascade Mountains are a new and jagged range, growing before our very eyes. The tectonic plate which holds North America grinds up and over the Pacific Ocean's Juan de Fuca plate a few centimeters each year. That's a brisk pace by our planet's standards. The stress buckles the Pacific Northwest upward, forming the Cascades. It also produces volcanoes, among them Mount Saint Helens, Oregon's Mount Hood, and the tallest mountain in the range, Mount Rainier.

I reflect that mountains are not just big in themselves, they make everything else bigger, as well. Weather gets more dire. Rain gets rainy-er. Daily temperatures swing wildly in the thin air. Early season snowstorms can close roads, strand people, even threaten lives.

My little car labored its way up slope after ever-steepening slope. Then I rounded a curve and there was Mount

Rainier itself, a glorious, gleaming wedge thrust up from dark lower slopes. Wrapped in a mantle of glaciers, its shoulders shone as though silvered by God. A wisp of cloud shaded the summit, as though it had caught on a peak while sailing past.

I wheeled into a strategically located turnout, got out, and snapped pictures. While I was doing this, a motor home grunted up the slope from the opposite direction and stopped a dozen yards away. A whole family emerged, pointing and talking. No smarter or less touristy than I, they also hauled out cameras, took turns posing, and snapped away with the mountain in the background.

What, I wondered, did First Nations and pioneers do before cameras were invented? How did they memorialize their first look at this glorious sight? Or did they just keep walking? Did that make the view any less amazing?

I climbed back into my car and wound on down the grade, along a deep canyon, then into Mount Rainier National Park. Douglas firs and spruces loomed over the highway, massively appropriate to the mountain. A light drizzle, mist with just a trace of muscle, began as I pulled into a campground.

I chose a site and once more hauled out my tent and gear. Huge logs lay on either side, and the soil felt spongy to the step, as though the ground itself was composed of deadfalls. I tied my lines off to convenient branches or drove spikes directly into those two pithy, fallen trunks.

Peering up between the soaring evergreens, I could just make out a shoulder of glacier above me. The sun had set down where I was, but it still gleamed off the ice farther up. The place gave me a funny feeling, beauty and danger mingled. I had read about the chance of avalanches on Mount Rainier, and passed signs marking, "Volcano Escape Route." I had even chosen my campsite with a view toward protection from possibly cascading boulders. Yet it was so gorgeous, so peaceful in the moment.

Back in the 1990s, the United Nations sponsored what was called the International Decade for Disaster Reduction. Part of this project involved study of volcanoes. Volcanologists listed sixteen volcanoes that were near populous areas and prone to frequent eruptions as "Decade Volcanoes." That is, they were so dangerous they needed constant monitoring. Now here I was, camped on the slope of the Decade Volcano known as Mount Rainier.

Mount St. Helens's 1980 eruption demonstrated what a Cascades volcano can do. But Mount St. Helens was relatively remote, most of its eruption spent on "empty" forest. Mount Rainier stands fifty miles from the Seattle megalopolis. Including my own children and grandchildren.

Mount Rainier has nothing to do with the Yellowstone Hot Spot. The Cascade volcanoes are all about continental drift, a separate process. Meanwhile, YouTube videos and breathless magazine articles flog the death-dealing potential. "Mount Rainier Is a ticking time bomb" one shouts. True, but not helpful.

Our relatively gentle planet is, well, only relatively gentle. Potential casualties from one or another of earth's burps range from Mount Rainier's tens of thousands of potential deaths, all the way up to the destruction of civilization as we know it. No kidding. No joke. We all live on the caldera, so to speak. We're all within reach of some geologic feature that could, with one heave, wipe out all we think we know.

One prior example in the geologic record is Mount Toba, a super volcano in Indonesia. It blew seventy thousand years ago, cremated five thousand square miles of terrain, and its ash blocked world sunlight for years. Global temperatures dropped, plant life wilted, and whole species became extinct. Genetic analysis indicates it also wiped out 90 percent of the human race at the time. Hug your loved ones today, and maybe even your enemies, because that one eruption brought us all within a whisker of not even being here.

The earth sleeps restlessly and has no remorse. Its stirrings are the stuff of apocalypse. The rest of the time, intervals equal to all of recorded human history, it feeds us, nurtures us, cradles us in her bosom. Each year brings a natural disaster or two, but destruction is confined to pockets. Earth sleeps today and we sleep as well. At least in the Zen Buddhist sense.

Mount St. Helens gave us a checklist for Mount Rainier's next eruption. Volcanic heat will melt Rainier's glaciers. Lahar mudflows will scour down the valleys at forty miles an hour toward Puget Sound, burying everything in their paths. Survivors will later analyze the death, destruction, and misery, and note that it was all as predictable as that dolomite ridge above Rock Creek Campground. Analysis done, predictability noted.

Yet there I was, setting up camp between two fallen Douglas firs on the mountain slope itself. Because a body has to sleep somewhere. I conclude that to live at all, is to tempt a volcano of one kind or another.

Evening drew on and cool mist thickened Mount Rainier's air. It wasn't quite rain, but almost. The layer of rotting wood beneath my campsite felt bouncy with metamorphosis. Darkness approached, laden with aromas of pine and campfire smoke. I set my goods out on a convenient picnic table and heated dinner on my propane stove. Below me, down the mountainside, I could hear the musical shouts of unseen children playing. Above me a national park sign pointed toward the nearest avalanche evacuation route. Only time and chance separated me from those campers in Rock Creek Campground.

I got a great night's sleep. Walking to and from my

morning compulsories at the campground bathroom, I passed other campers. They mostly spoke English, but I also heard German and another language I couldn't name. I felt awash in the luxury of twenty-first-century outdoors.

I found out, several days later, that my daughter's friend-of-a-friend had made his annual birthday ascent of Mount Rainier that same week. Dormant volcano though it is, Rainier is known for frequent small earthquakes on its upper slopes. I never thought about that, sleeping lower down. But as this group made their way toward the summit, a tremor sent boulders bouncing down the steep slope. The rest of the party got out of the way and were unharmed, but a boulder struck the birthday hiker and killed him. The body had to be evacuated by helicopter.

I spent my night in the presence of death, in the web of death's beauty, quite unaware. I touched the tip of this mountain's finger. At the same time, farther up the slope, it was flicking off a human life the way you'd flick a careless bug. Park authorities say several people a year get killed that way.

Around the world, scientists use technology to peer into the hearts of Mount Rainier, Mount St. Helens, Yellowstone, Toba, Tambora, Santorini, on and on. Any of them, on a geologic whim, could deal death to multitudes. We're learning their ways, but they do not change their millennial nature.

It's all related, we live on more brinks than just volcanoes. Cultural devastation is not just someone else's possibility. Excepting a hiccup here and there, life allows people like me to sleep peacefully, each after our own manner, centuries at a time. But North America's indigenous peoples faced one such hiccup, the colonial European avalanche. Other nemeses wait in the form of accumulated waste, accumulated damage to earth's systems—or the next great outburst of earth itself. When that avalanche comes, Euro-American culture may have a chance to experience survivance from the inside.

I ponder these things in my heart. I give thanks for the privilege of coming this way. I'm thankful to have read Plenty Coups and Pretty Shield, Jonathan Lear and Fujitaro Kubota. For now, appreciation holds off foreboding. But we need to learn the lessons offered to us. We need to learn the subtlety of triumph when the world has stripped away what we think is ours. Because our children, or perhaps our grandchildren's grandchildren, will survive or not, according to those techniques.

And another day's driving brought me to family and a regular bed.

MISTER KUBOTA'S GARDEN

cool Seattle weekday finds me in the bosom of family. My life partner, Kate, has flown in to join me. We are with my elder daughter Erin, her younger sister, Colleen, Colleen's husband, Matthew, and their two children. Moira, the girl, is three, old enough to run. Baby Quinn is still in arms. They are my tiny corner of the gene pool.

We are touring Seattle's Kubota Garden, the thirty-acre reflective space built by Fujitaro Kubota and his sons. It has the peaceful Zen spirit I expected, but also the childlike exuberance of a Suzuki violin concert. Watching little kids run around in a place like this lends a feathered edge to my appreciation. The "camp" at Minidoka seems far away. But it tints the mental lens through which I view this day. Fujitaro Kubota suffered and survived, built and rebuilt this nurturing space.

It strikes me that both survivance and being a nurse log contain kindred energy. They are not strangers, but lovers. This is important to me. Dominant culture must be respectful in its terminology. African American, First Nation, BGLTQ folk, any number of our culture's subsets, understand such words as "resistance," "resilience," and "survivance" in a way a straight, white male such as myself can only appreciate in the abstract. At the same time, survivance and the aspiration to be a nurse log live in relationship. And will grow closer with time. I now see part of my work as furthering that amalgamation.

We cross a glistening watercourse, stepping gingerly on broad stones. We stretch out hands to steady one another. Moira takes her father's hand reluctantly, then as soon as she's across, lets go and speeds up the path. Looking out from his baby carrier, Quinn has no opinion. His mother, my daughter, still tires easily. She accepts every hand she gets, and sits where sitting is available.

The brochure tells us Kubota Garden is a blend of traditional Japanese gardening techniques combined with plants and materials natural to the Puget Sound area. Plus a dose of whimsy. Fujitaro Kubota was not trained in the art of Japanese gardening. He immigrated to the United States to work on America's railroads and only later found his gift for gardening. He bought a piece of what was then swampland in southeast Seattle, used most of it for his nursery, and started this garden on the remainder in 1927. He is credited for bringing traditional Japanese gardening to the United States, adapting to the plants and conditions he found here.

That was before the US government decided Japanese Americans on the West Coast were dangerous. Mister Kubota and hundreds of his neighbors took their four-year hiatus, cultivating someone else's sugar beets on Idaho's high desert.

You'd never guess it, looking out over Kubota Garden. The place is full of joyful exuberance, the kind of fierce gentleness that keeps survivance alive when mere resistance goes down fighting. The Kubotas' perseverance dissolves both white suspicion and Japanese American pain in floral riches. "This is who we are," it seems to say, sustained by folkways of their own. And who they are is ineffably greater than what was done to them.

I humbly accept the gift without losing focus on what's going on here. Japanese youth humbled themselves to fight and die for the nation that imprisoned their parents. Crow youth joined that same army, as Joseph Medicine Crow put it, "to give back." They refused to be lessened by oppression, even to the point of risking life and limb for the oppressors' children. I'm grasping here. I sense something on which, as a privileged white male, I cannot get a clean grip. Perhaps I would feel it better if Plenty Coups came and laughed and touched me on the shoulder with his cane.

Meanwhile, the spirit of Kubota Garden manifests as a wrap-around nurse log. Moira and Quinn are every toddler and every infant who ever lived. For an instant, Moira becomes the imp-goddess of muddy boots, running ahead, then scrambling back to grab her father's arm and dragging him to show off an insect tasting a blossom. Galloping free once more, she slows only long enough to stomp her way through a convenient mud puddle.

There are multiple large koi ponds. The first time Moira sees one, she stretches out on a rock beside the water, reaches as far as she can. She dangles a finger for the koi to come nibble—and one does! She then repeats the gesture at every koi pond she sees. She is creativity in process, fermenting an adult who will someday be someone we didn't predict. At the age of three, her creative process has no back side.

We follow labyrinthine paths, separating, then coming back together as tracks rejoin. Fragrances drift on us like subtle blessings. We wind toward a different waterway where the path crosses a Guzei, the red, rounded bridge ubiquitous in Japanese gardens. This one is particularly steep and challenging. It is, the literature says, a symbolic crossing from the realm of the physical to the realm of spirit. It's steep going up because of the difficulty of the transition, and steep going down because of the richness by which the spirit feeds us. Living a good life is difficult, it says. It's tricky to walk up. It's tricky to walk down. I suspect Fujitaro Kubota would know.

Moira makes exaggerated groans going up one side, then thunders like a herd of buffalo down the other. The momentum carries her down the path till she's almost out of sight.

More paths lead us back uphill toward the wall and gatehouse area. I read that the wall, a later addition, is made of stones stacked without mortar. It is designed so that the stones' natural weight forces them ever more firmly against one another. Even the shaking of an earthquake will only make the wall stronger.

I reflect that sometimes human beings are the earthquake. Sometimes, bless our hearts, we're the wall.

Radical hope. Crazy Horse, Sitting Bull, even Custer, all went down fighting. I ache for the real suffering of the Kubota family during the Second World War. And their bad memories ever after. Yet their sensitivity in building Kubota Gardens effectively discarded that oppression in a dump of irrelevance. That's power. Giving one's best to the society which had taken away so much. The Crow soldiers fighting on the same front as the Nisei would understand. Survivance lies in knowing when to bring-together rather than tear-apart.

FIDELITY TO HOPE

A year after my rolling spiritual retreat, Donald Trump found himself, to his apparent surprise and everyone else's, elected President. That political sea change led to many of my fellow white liberals calling themselves, "The Resistance." This is okay as political theatre, I guess. But do we really take the word resistance seriously?

Can we compare ourselves to, say, French or Dutch resistance under Nazi occupation? Or Jews uprising in the Warsaw Ghetto? Or the heroic-but-futile resistance of Sitting Bull and Crazy Horse? They faced death and knew it. Not just their own deaths, either, but the likely deaths of loved ones and all else they held dear.

When Euro-Americans like me claim the mantle of resistance, what do we risk?

I do agree, future generations face dire consequences from actions and processes now unfolding. But what is it, exactly, that we say we're "resisting?" A political party? A set of officials or policies we despise? What if people of my political persuasion win the next election? What does resistance become after that happens? Is it a rhetorical tool, to be discarded once the "right" people are back in charge? If that happens—and I think it will—it will say something profound about what's being called "resistance" in this moment.

Without question, we are looking at a future full of doubt. That begs the question, what does radical hope look like in our time? What does the achievable victory look like? Answers to all those questions must come from a place deeper and more profound than political slogans.

This is not to say evocative words cannot be used. It is, however, to say that a claim of powerful words ought to touch a powerful reality. We shortchange ourselves and others unless we take seriously the ground in which our words are planted.

To put it a different way, the subtle strategies of Plenty Coups and his fellow elders produced real victories. But their circumstances made those victories limited ones, which they had to learn to accept. Meanwhile the outright resistance of Crazy Horse and Sitting Bull left them dead and their people, in Plenty Coups' words, "hating the land that held their lodges."

It didn't play out that way simply because Plenty Coups was smart while Crazy Horse and Sitting Bull were not. Rather, the Crow and Lakota Nations were responding out of starkly different life situations.

When Crazy Horse and Sitting Bull were born, the Lakota were the most powerful of the plains Nations. Lakota resistance was the reaction of a people who, for the first time, faced an enemy stronger than they were.

Though courageous and proud, the Crow had been hard-pressed, fighting for survival, for a generation by the time Plenty Coups was born. They had already begun to adapt their strategies to their disadvantage. Two Nations reacted differently because they were faced with different world views.

Later, as their fates became common, their practice of survivance became common as well. Nor, in this century, are indigenous peoples the only disadvantaged ethnicity who have learned skills of patience, subtlety, commonality, and the limited victory. Though the word, "survivance," is peculiar to indigenous experience, I suggest that the practice itself is common to many peoples who face Euro-American cultural dominance.

I have to wonder, therefore, does talk of "resistance" and "revolution" among progressive Euro-Americans merely reflect socio-economic privilege and control which, for all our good intentions, we can't imagine ourselves being without?

I cannot practice survivance. A person like me has not lived that necessity. A black youth facing a St. Louis patrolman, say, needs the subtlety of survivance without ever having heard the word. That youth's parents profoundly pray he understands as much. The First Nations who gathered at the Missouri River to denounce the Dakota Access Pipeline, they knew. The First Nations who already look ahead to the next consumer culture attack on their rights and resources, they know.

The past is not amenable to change. I'm not sure about the future. We can, at least, try to be honest with ourselves. And practice humility. Ally is an important word, But I believe that Euro-American allies like me need to learn from those to whom we say we're allied. The oppressed, it seems to me, understand both resistance and commonality in ways more profound than those who peer from relative privilege. Children of colonizers may function without understanding the colonized, or even themselves. For the oppressed not to understand the oppressors—is suicidal. Ask the Ghost Dancers.

I also learn from Jonathan Lear's *Radical Hope*, a philosopher translating survivance into Euro-American terms without ever having heard the word. Resilience, generosity, commonality, and the subtle art of the achievable victory. Those, if I read him right, are key markers toward what he calls radical hope.

Jonathan Lear closes his book with a pithy analysis on what he calls fidelity to hope. He contrasts between Plenty Coups and the better known visionary, Wovoka. Wovoka and his followers dreamed that Ghost Dancing would make the whites disappear and bring back the buffalo and the old ways of life. The changes and losses of the age would, in their belief, simply reverse themselves. We see how that worked out. Fidelity to hope, then, is to accept one's limited social means without losing resolve to work hard for all that can be achieved.

Wovoka's preaching reminds me of some liberal "revolution" rhetoric in our own time. Meanwhile, "Make America Great Again," it seems to me, calls us back to a Euro-American world dominance that always existed more as comfortable myth than as reality. It certainly reveals a reactionary yearning for a time before most Euro-Americans worried about common humanity or the shadow side of technology.

Delusion abounds on all sides. Because we abhor the boring, often distasteful work of politics, much of the voting public condemns even the most capable or honest politicians. Meanwhile we rhapsodize shining-but-unaccomplished icons of liberal purity on the left and authoritarian flame-throwers on the right.

Is this political malaise part of a greater debility? I see our very democracy staggering beneath the weight of a cultural addiction to convenience. We eschew the unending, day-to-day struggle. We have no eye to recognize incremental and imperfect labor toward difficult, long-range goals. I watch as some Euro-Americans decry any perceived loss of real privilege, no matter how slight, as suffering equal to the Lakota at Wounded Knee or captured Africans at an antebellum slave auction.

Plenty Coups and his village elders charted a course that realistically accepted their misfortune, striving to mitigate it wherever they could. They steered a thoughtful course between shoals on all sides: surrender, Wovoka's magical thinking, the equally deadly resolve to "go down fighting."

As I write, hurricanes of unprecedented power ravage America's East Coast. Wildfires of the same nature ravage the West. I wonder if Euro-American culture is feeling the first zephyrs of a whirlwind of its own creation. When our cultural devastation comes, and it will come, more will be lost than just comfort and social privilege. What, then, might be the native folkway by which we might persist and evolve? We will have one another, sons and daughters of our fellow women and men. I return to survivance as communal practice. If we're really lucky, will we have learned to partner in ways we have not yet foreseen?

Can we learn to practice such an ethic as prevention rather than cure?

Late in life, Plenty Coups "converted" from his traditional religion to Roman Catholicism. Reading his words, I take it that he was not putting down one religion to pick up a different one, but *widening* his religious circle to the maximum possible. It's possible that he did have, in the back of his mind, one more strategy to open the white mind to Crow reality. But his words strike me as sincere, speaking of a spirituality which took in both Catholicism and his indigenous religious practice.

Can religion, in the broadest sense, be a common folkway by which we might begin to transcend our challenges? This would require a *religion of radical hope*—survivance—that sees the human commonality lying beneath doctrine and tradition. It requires religious sensitivity founded in common humanity and the moment-by-moment work of each day. A few religious expressions have taken tentative steps in that direction. But it is a difficult discipline. Can we recognize our differences as the imaginary things they are? Or will we perish in our separate, mutually paranoid, groups?

Our grandchildren and their grandchildren will look back on us through the mists of time. They must live with the result of our work.

Pretty Shield's father knew something which, I believe, we need to take seriously. His religion doesn't strike me as what he *believed* nearly as much as the way he *allowed himself to be changed by the sacred he saw all around him*. May we learn from him and from one another. May we learn, figuratively, to "sit and smoke" with one another and with the wonderful and terrible physical miracle of the world in which we dwell.

POSTSCRIPT: CLOUDS

*T*he little girl, Moira, is strapped into her child seat in the back of her parents' car. They're driving to a park near their apartment where they will meet other parents and children for a play date. It's a gorgeous Seattle summer day. The sky is robin's-egg blue. Cumulous clouds drift overhead in fleecy squadrons.

"Those clouds are beautiful," Moira's mother says, looking back at the child. "That one looks like a lady smiling. See it, Moira?"

From the back seat, Moira laughs. "Pretty clouds," she says. Then after a thoughtful silence, she says, "Mommy, are clouds soft?"

"They're really, really soft. Softer than anything."

"I'm going to bring you some clouds."

Her mother smiles, a tidbit of delight. "You are? How are you going to get them?"

"I'll need a good ladder," Moira says, her thinking stretched beyond simple physics. "You'll have to help me set up the ladder."

Moira's mother and father glance at one another.

"I'll need special gloves, too," Moira says. "Special gloves will

289

keep the cloud-stuff from sticking to my hands. And I'll need some kind of a bag to put the clouds in."

As do we all.

ABOUT THE AUTHOR

Dennis McCarty has lived a richly varied life. Over the decades he has written well-reviewed novels, plays, and songs, worked in heavy construction, and taught overseas. He went into Unitarian Universalist ministry in 1998. Though retired from parish ministry, he still speaks in churches around the country. He also presents a one-person version of his play, *Servetus: the Radical Reformed Musical.*

Dennis is Minister Emeritus at the Unitarian Universalist Congregation of Columbus, Indiana. He has two accomplished adult daughters, Erin and Colleen, and two grandchildren, Moira and Quinn. He lives in Bloomington, Indiana, with his life partner, Kate, and two pampered cats, Gandhi and Dora the Explorer.

Made in the USA
Middletown, DE
05 September 2023